NEPANTLA

An Anthology for Queer Poets of Color

T0153409

NEPANTLA

An Anthology for Queer Poets of Color

Edited by Christopher Soto

Nightboat Books
New York

©2018 by Nightboat Books
Introduction and Editing © 2018 by Christopher Soto
All rights reserved
Printed in the United States
Sixth Printing, 2023

ISBN: 978-1-937658-78-6

Interior design & typesetting by HR Hegnauer
Text set in Perpetua and Calibri
Cover Design by Irmand Trujillo
Cover Image by Irmand Trujillo, "Obsidian Automatic," 2016
Courtesy of the artist

This publication was produced in conjunction with Lambda Literary.

LAMBDA LITERARY is the leading national nonprofit for LGBTQ readers, writers, publishers, editors, librarians, booksellers and the entire LGBTQ literary community. We believe that lesbian, gay, bisexual, transgender, and queer literature is fundamental to the preservation of our culture, and that LGBTQ lives are affirmed when our stories are written, published, and read.

LAMBDA
LITERARY

Cataloging-in-publication data is available from the Library of Congress

Nightboat Books
New York
www.nightboat.org

Dedicated to
William Johnson & Lambda Literary

CHRISTOPHER SOTO

Introduction

In 2013, I founded *Nepantla* as an online journal with Lambda Literary. The mission of the journal was to nurture, celebrate, and preserve diversity within the queer poetry community. The journal existed online for three years and in that time frame it gained the attention of thousands of readers internationally. With the guidance and support of William Johnson at Lambda Literary, I helped *Nepantla* quickly become a refuge for some of the most prominent queer of color poets in the United States. In 2017, Nightboat Books and I entered into conversation and thus this anthology began production. The title of the journal and (subsequently) this anthology are derived from a quote by Gloria E. Anzaldúa's *This Bridge We Call Home:*

> Bridges are thresholds to other realities, archetypal, primal symbols of shifting consciousness. They are passageways, conduits, and connectors that connote transitioning, crossing borders, and changing perspectives. Bridges span liminal (threshold) spaces between worlds, spaces I call *nepantla*, a Nahuatl word meaning *tierra entre medio*. Transformations occur in this in-between space, an unstable, unpredictable, precarious, always-in-transition space lacking clear boundaries. *Nepantla es tierra desconocida*, and living in this liminal zone means being in a constant state of displacement—an uncomfortable, even alarming feeling. Most of us dwell in *nepantla* so much of the time it's become a sort of "home." Though this state links us to other ideas, people, and worlds, we feel threatened by these new connections and the change they engender.

The title of this book, *Nepantla*, is meant to connote a transient feeling—the feeling of shifting between various communities and identities. This sentiment has also been echoed by Dr. José Esteban Muñoz in *Disidentifications* where he writes, "[Queer of color] subjects' different identity components occupy adjacent spaces and are not comfortably situated in any one discourse of minority subjectivity. These hybridized identificatory positions are always in transit, shuttling between different identity vectors." The contents of *Nepantla* span a moderate amount of time and space. The earliest poets in this anthology are from the Harlem Renaissance in the 1920s and other poets in this anthology are just beginning their lives and careers. Approximately 100 years of poetry are fit into these pages. That being said, many voices are missing from this anthology too. One book can't contain all queer of color literary history. I view this anthology as another addition to the conversation, a testament to our continuing legacy.

As an anthology, *Nepantla* is interested in critical intellectual, emotional, and artistic inquiry. The poems selected in the anthology were published based on three primary factors: What is at the emotional core of the poem? What is at stake within the content of the poem? Has the poet been absolutely pivotal to development of other queer of color poets? This anthology is not interested in overly crafted poems or political perfection. The poems in this anthology grapple with a variety of issues, most obviously: race, gender, and sexual orientation. Also discussed are police violence, riots, body image, kink, food, joy, religion, and more. The content and form of the poems in this anthology are as diverse as the people who created them.

With the belief that constructive criticism can be beneficial, the following are some limitations to the anthology. (1) To state that something is the "first major" anthology can be dangerous. What if there is another anthology for queer poets of color in the United States that we somehow have not heard of? (2) The title of this anthology references Gloria E. Anzaldúa whose notions of mestizaje are currently being heavily debated in academia. What if *Nepantla* should not have been used as the title? (3) Notions about who constitutes as people of color are also questionable. If someone is Native American, how does the term "people of color" operate from the colonial gaze? (4) When this anthology is read by people who are based outside of the United States, can that be a form of pink-washing and imposing contemporary American understandings of gender and sexuality onto other places? (5) This anthology did not publish poets prior to the Harlem Renaissance because definitions of gender and sexuality have shifted so drastically over centuries. (6) How is the word "queer" also an inaccurate description of poets included in this anthology? It may have been more accurate to list: queer, trans, gender non-conforming, intersex, etc. (7) Not everyone in this anthology may have identified exactly as a queer person of color. Yet, everyone in this anthology has likely been perceived as, or perceived themselves as, both non-white and a gender or sexual minority.

Considering the limitations, I still believe this anthology is a necessity because the ever shifting boundaries of language around race, gender, and sexuality have affected the material realities faced by many minority subjects. This anthology provides an important space to reflect on the lives of those of us who have lived on the outskirts of what is deemed acceptable or respectable.

NEPANTLA

PAT PARKER

Don't Let The Fascists Speak

"Don't let the fascists speak."
"We want to hear what they have to say."
"Keep them out of the classroom."
"Everybody is entitled to freedom of speech."

I am a child of America
a step child
    raised in the back room
yet taught
    taught how to act
in her front room.
my mind jumps
the voices of students
screaming
insults   threats
"Let the Nazis speak"
"Let the Nazis speak"
Everyone is entitled
    to speak
I sit a greasy-legged
    Black child
in a Black school
in the Black part of town
look to the Black teacher
The Bill of Rights
    guarantees
us all the right
    my mind

remembers   chants
article I article I
& my innards churn
they remember
the Black teacher
in the Black school
in the Black part
of the very white town
who stopped us
when we attacked
the puppet principal
the white Board
of mis-Education
cast-off books
illustrated with
cartoons &
words of wisdom
written by white
children in the
other part of town
missing pages
caricatures
of hanging niggers—
the bill of rights
was written to
        protect
            us

my mind remembers
& my innards churn
conjures images
            police
break up

illegal demonstrations
illegal assemblies
        conjures images
of a Black Panther
"if tricky Dick
tried to stop us
we'll stop him"
conjure image
of that same Black man
going to jail
for threatening
the life of
        THE PRESIDENT
every citizen
is entitled to
freedom of speech
my mind remembers
& my innards churn
conjure images
of jews in camps
of homosexuals in camps
of socialists in camps
"Let the Nazis speak"
"Let the Nazis speak"
        faces in a college
          classroom
"You're being fascist too."
"We want to hear what
they have to say"

        faces in
a college classroom
young white faces
        speak let them speak

speak let them speak
Blacks, jews, some whites
seize the bullhorn
"We don't want to hear
your socialist rhetoric"
        socialist rhetoric
        survival
            rhetoric
the supreme court
says it is illegal
to scream fire
in a crowded theater

to scream fire
in a crowded theater
causes people to panic
to run to hurt each other
my mind remembers
& now I know
what my innards
        say
illegal to cause
        people
to panic
to run
to hurt
there is
no contradiction
what the Nazis say
will cause
        people
        to hurt
        ME.

DENICE FROHMAN

once a marine biologist
told me octopuses have three hearts

I wonder what I'd do
    with eight arms, two eyes
        & too many ways to give
            myself away

        see, I only have one heart
        & I know loving a woman can make you crawl
    out from under yourself, or forget
the kingdom that is your body

& what would you say, octopus?
    that you live knowing nobody
        can touch you more
            than you do already

        that you can't punch anything underwater
    so you might as well drape yourself
        around it, bring it right up to your mouth
    let each suction cup kiss what it finds

        that having this many hands
    means to hold everything
  at once & nothing
to hold you back

that when you split
   you turn your blood
      blue & pour
         out more ocean

            that you know heartbreak so well
         you remove all your bones
   so nothing can kill you.

I haven't had a Sazerac since Indiana

nor loved a white
woman. Admittedly

I am drawn
to its complexity

but then always
that insidious

aftertaste
like anise

to make me doubt
how long I can

hold you in my mouth.

OCEAN VUONG

Someday I'll Love Ocean Vuong

After Frank O'Hara / After Roger Reeves

Ocean, don't be afraid.
The end of the road is so far ahead
it is already behind us.
Don't worry. Your father is only your father
until one of you forgets. Like how the spine
won't remember its wings
no matter how many times our knees
kiss the pavement. Ocean,
are you listening? The most beautiful part
of your body is wherever
your mother's shadow falls.
Here's the house with childhood
whittled down to a single red tripwire.
Don't worry. Just call it *horizon*
& you'll never reach it.
Here's today. Jump. I promise it's not
a lifeboat. Here's the man
whose arms are wide enough to gather
your leaving. & here the moment,
just after the lights go out, when you can still see
the faint torch between his legs.
How you use it again & again
to find your own hands.
You asked for a second chance
& are given a mouth to empty out of.

Don't be afraid, the gunfire
is only the sound of people
trying to live a little longer
& failing. Ocean. Ocean—
get up. The most beautiful part of your body
is where it's headed. & remember,
loneliness is still time spent
with the world. Here's
the room with everyone in it.
Your dead friends passing
through you like wind
through a wind chime. Here's a desk
with the gimp leg & a brick
to make it last. Yes, here's a room
so warm & blood-close,
I swear, you will wake—
& mistake these walls
for skin.

Poem about Police Violence

Tell me something
what you think would happen if
everytime they kill a black boy
then we kill a cop
everytime they kill a black man
then we kill a cop

you think the accident rate would lower subsequently?
sometimes the feeling like amaze me baby
comes back to my mouth and I am quiet
like Olympian pools from the running
mountainous snows under the sun

sometimes thinking about the 12th House of the Cosmos
or the way your ear ensnares the tip
of my tongue or signs that I have never seen
like DANGER WOMEN WORKING

I lose consciousness of ugly bestial rapid
and repetitive affront as when they tell me
18 cops in order to subdue one man
18 strangled him to death in the ensuing scuffle
(don't you idolize the diction of the powerful: *subdue*
and *scuffle* my oh my) and that the murder
that the killing of Arthur Miller on a Brooklyn
street was just a "justifiable accident" again
(Again)

People been having accidents all over the globe
so long like that I reckon that the only
suitable insurance is a gun
I'm saying war is not to understand or rerun
war is to be fought and won

sometimes the feeling like amaze me baby
blots it out/the bestial but
not too often tell me something
what you think would happen if
everytime they kill a black boy
then we kill a cop
everytime they kill a black man
then we kill a cop

you think the accident rate would lower subsequently

The [Black]Outs : Listen

Elegy with My Mother's Lipstick

I climb down to the beach facing the Pacific Ocean. Torrents of rain
shirr the sand. On the other side, my grandmother sleeps soundlessly
in her bed. Her áo dài of the whitest silk. My mother knew her mother
died before the telephone rang like bells announcing the last American
helicopter leaving Sài Gòn. Arrow shot back to its bow, long-distance
missile: she'd leap into the sky to fly home if she could. She works
overtime instead. Curls her hair with hot rollers. Rouges her cheeks
like Gong Li in *Raise the Red Lantern*. And I'm her understudy. Hiding
in the doorways between her grief and mine, I apply her foundation
to my face. I conceal the parts of me she conceals, puckering my lips
as if to kiss a man that loves me the way I want to be loved. I speak
their bewitching names aloud: *Twisted Rose, Fuchsia in Paris, Irreverence.*
I choose the lipstick she'd least approve. My mouth a pomegranate
split open, a grenade with its loose pin. In the kitchen, I wrap a sheet
around my waist and dance for hours, mesmerized by my reflection
in a charred skillet. I laugh her laugh, the way my grandmother laughed
as she taught me to pray the Chú Đại Bi. I remember braiding her hair
in unbearable heat. My tiny fingers weaving silver strands into a fishtail,
a French twist. Each knot a future she never named, buried in the soil
of her, the barren plot where she keeps the image of invaders locking
her sons away. I'm sorry, mother of my mother, immortal bodhisattva
with a thousand hands, chewing a fist of betel root, your teeth black
as dawn. No child in our family stays a child their mother can love.

Riot Act, April 29, 1992

I'm going out and get something.
I don't know what.
I don't care.
Whatever's out there, I'm going to get it.
Look in those shop windows at boxes
and boxes of Reeboks and Nikes
to make me fly through the air
like Michael Jordan
like Magic.
While I'm up there, I see Spike Lee.

Looks like he's flying too
straight through the glass
that separates me
from the virtual reality
I watch everyday on TV.
I know the difference between
what it is and what it isn't.
Just because I can't touch it
doesn't mean it isn't real.
All I have to do is smash the screen,
reach in and take what I want.
Break out of prison.
South Central homey newly risen
from the night of living dead,
but this time he lives,
he gets to give the zombies

a taste of their own medicine.
Open wide and let me in,
or else I'll set your world on fire,
but you pretend that you don't hear.
You haven't heard the word is coming down
like the hammer of the gun
of this black son, locked out of the big house,
while massa looks out the window and sees only smoke.
Massa doesn't see anything else,
not because he can't,
but because he won't.
He'd rather hear me talking about mo' money,

mo' honeys and gold chains
and see me carrying my favorite things
from looted stores
than admit that underneath my Raider's cap,
the aftermath is staring back
unblinking through the camera's lens,
courtesy of CNN,
my arms loaded with boxes of shoes
that I will sell at the swap meet
to make a few cents on the declining dollar.
And if I destroy myself
and my neighborhood
"ain't nobody's business if I do,"
but the police are knocking hard
at my door
and before I can open it,
they break it down
and drag me in the yard.
They take me in to be processed and charged,

to await trial,
while Americans forget
the day the wealth finally trickled down
to the rest of us.

Power

The difference between poetry and rhetoric
is being ready to kill
yourself
instead of your children.

I am trapped on a desert of raw gunshot wounds
and a dead child dragging his shattered black
face off the edge of my sleep
blood from his punctured cheeks and shoulders
is the only liquid for miles
and my stomach
churns at the imagined taste while
my mouth splits into dry lips
without loyalty or reason
thirsting for the wetness of his blood
as it sinks into the whiteness
of the desert where I am lost
without imagery or magic
trying to make power out of hatred and destruction
trying to heal my dying son with kisses
only the sun will bleach his bones quicker.

A policeman who shot down a ten year old in Queens
stood over the boy with his cop shoes in childish blood
and a voice said "Die you little motherfucker" and
there are tapes to prove it. At his trial
this policeman said in his own defense

"I didn't notice the size nor nothing else
only the color". And
there are tapes to prove that, too.

Today that 37 year old white man
with 13 years of police forcing
was set free
by eleven white men who said they were satisfied
justice had been done
and one Black Woman who said
"They convinced me" meaning
they had dragged her 4'10'' black Woman's frame
over the hot coals
of four centuries of white male approval
until she let go
the first real power she ever had
and lined her own womb with cement
to make a graveyard for our children.

I have not been able to touch the destruction
within me.
But unless I learn to use
the difference between poetry and rhetoric
my power too will run corrupt as poisonous mold
or lie limp and useless as an unconnected wire
and one day I will take my teenaged plug
and connect it to the nearest socket
raping an 85 year old white woman
who is somebody's mother
and as I beat her senseless and set a torch to her bed
a greek chorus will be singing in 3/4 time
"Poor thing. She never hurt a soul. What beasts they are."

RONALDO V. WILSON

EXCERPT FROM Dream Vision in Blue and Black

Before breakfast at Jake's, on the benches outside, a little blue boy sees Virgil sketching, and asks him if he can look in his book. Virgil is generous, and opens his pad, leafing through the pages for the boy and his Mom/Aunt/or Guardian to see. The little blue boy does listen to his advice, nods his head when Virgil tells him that it's okay to "mess up." The Mom/Aunt/ or Guardian co-signs Virgil's recommendation, and they both follow along as Virgil slowly turns his pages, describing how, in one, he scraped all of the paint off with his Costco card to reveal the original marks, a flat black figure in magenta, a white man's face, caught by water-soluble pink oil pastel.

Virgil, as ever, is invested in the capture of depth's solitary surface. Though he isn't a lone wolf, he understands that "performing" as one who is alone garners his unique relationship to being isolated among others. For Virgil, this is a kind of first source, and from this source, he tries to explain to Music that Western Mass has never looked so beautiful to him before now. The trees are so wet and present, no monolithic vastness that can simply be read as "field." But still, they appear as full, thick and singular, like one green corridor he jogs through.

But in looking up, Virgil realizes any sense of actual height is too tall to track. When he lived closer to these trees, he was only familiar with existing above them, driving Desiré on US 90—like Manitoba, but much more affordable, and "Knowledge" Blue not "Passion" Red—through the mountains looking up at them, so that the trees were only texture.

feeding me starving

"i used to be
245" he tells me
like my middle
school husky pants is i
guess a lot to
weigh and lifts his
shirt, puts my
hand on his
soft flat stomach,
says "i want it
a little harder," asks
me what size
shirt i wear and how
much i weigh
i only know
the answer to
one of these questions,
tells me "i'm
gonna make you bigger,"
gets on top and puts his
dainty danish, tiny tart in my
mouth, just before his tongue,
a garnish of delight and approval i could
feast on forever, no
calories and
later (when i've
left and this is no

longer hot) i wonder
why he wants
to make me fatter
and shrink himself, what
am i ingesting that
is just his digestion,
baby bird of
desperation and no self-love
so i can
be his hard
-on in the sheets and harassed in the
streets, effigy of disgust and
confusion, so he can
be lean and
hot, "verse, but i
only top chubs"
thinness and penetration don't have to
be about power but why does this make
me feel so dis(sed)empowered and
who is fucking him when
he's not fucking me and what's
their shirt size, how thin do you have to be
to be loved
and when
will he text
me back i'm
hungry

Quantitative Reasoning

1

I don't know how much more coleslaw I can take.

2

& I love coleslaw.

3

If Brian is traveling at 71 miles per hour & Ryan is traveling at 74 miles per hour & a dog is barking at another dog for 7 dog minutes, when would be the best time for me to visit you?

4

My boyfriend Jeff routinely gets his younger sister's age wrong. My mother always mixes up my two younger brothers in their baby pictures. These are the mistakes we like to laugh about.

5

Which amount is greater?
A) The electrons in your left foot
B) God's pinkie finger
C) What you wished you had room for last week at Old
    Country Buffet

6

I find myself envious of Jeff for getting to have a relationship with my mother that doesn't involve the last twenty years. They can just talk about cats & how to bake different things better. Then I think of Jeff saying that it's a good thing I met

his family now. After all the divorce & marrying new people &
buying new houses.

7

It's never too late for someone else to have your happy childhood.

8

To determine how old my father is, I always have to add five
years to my mother's age. Plus five years of the hair dye I will
probably use, too.

9

On a scale of 1 to lenticular cloud, what is the median household
height of a lonely child's imaginary friend, a friend whose name
has remained a well-guarded secret, even after x as well as y
amount of years?

Layover

Dallas is so far away
Even for the people who live
In Dallas is Dallas far away
A hub
Through which we get
To smaller places
That lurch and hurt
Mean stopping
In Dallas and all are
From small towns and farms
If all keep going
Back far enough
Pay attention
Keep your belongings near
Everyone in Dallas
Is still driving
At 3:24 a.m. off I-20
Where I was raped
Though no one
Would call it that
He was inside
By the time I realized
He thought it necessary
To leave me with knowledge
I can be hated
I was smaller then
One road went through me

No airport
I drove him home
There had been a wreck
On the interstate
I sat in traffic
My wallet on the seat
In between my legs.

Hurryer ___ thruu [--------- ...... ++++]

Grenada. Grenade. What isn't wearing
fur in our backless
back-ordered, addressed and reboardered

grmmattic; birth—a—stroll again

st—reek of it. Strut_strut_strip, maul / -iver-oil

y we ween an endgame from our touristician clm

up to famino / acidic / ha, couldn't you

predict it? History, fortune, eastern religions: &lso

3 kinds of geometry so far

& no new polygon for living? Trapezoid, anachronistic lapse

enjoyed too often—ah. Say open. Say machinery if empathy

when iron or deficiency. Clutch fever for river fervor for_ what_

On Grace

For Tim Seibles, Ross Gay, Kevin Simmonds, & Pages Matam

You know how when Usain Bolt runs
& you want to cry it's so beautiful? That.

How could we not be a song? I hum
this man in my bed all night, my mouth a loose choir

& his body a gospel & I don't mean like a song
I mean gospel like a religion or like a testimony

etched in gold. How could we be *only* a song?
I lay men down for what some call me a faggot for

but I call it *worship*, I see his wood & bark
Amen Amen Amen. I call out God's good name

in the midst of the first miracle—the black body.
Look at him, at us. Were the mountains not named

after some dark brotha's shoulders? Didn't the wind learn
its ways from watching two boys run the spine of a field?

Bless the birch-colored body, always threatening to grow
or burn. Bless the body that strikes fear in pale police

& wets the mouths of church girls & choir boys with want.
Am I allowed to say I praised my pastor most without the robe?

I have found God in the saltiest parts of men: the space between
the leg & what biology calls a man, the bottoms of feet, life's slow milk.

I watch the Heat play the Warriors & I am overcome by a need
for tears & teeth. I stopped playing football because being tackled

feels too much like making love. I pause in the middle of the street
watching the steady pace of the men on corners selling green

& all things dangerous & white. I watch the hands exchange money
& escape, the balancing act of hips & denim. This awful dance of poverty,

but the dancers? Tatted & callous ballerinas, henna dipped stars.
Do you know what it means to be that beautiful & still hunted

& still alive? Who knows this story but the elephants & the trees?
Who says the grace of a black man in motion is not perfect

as a tusk in the sun or a single leaf taking its sweet time to the ground?

ADRIAN STANFORD

for stan

i guess i love you,
so much unsaid we seem
to understand
we have lived in our short years,
but it has not been a life of love
i am old before my time,
and yet it is good to be with you
so there is hope for me i guess,
i love you

MARCELO HERNANDEZ CASTILLO

Cenzóntle

Because the bird flew before
    there was a word
    for flight

        years from now
        there will be a name
      for what you and I are doing.

I licked the mango of the sun—

between its bone and its name
between its color and its weight,

    the night was heavier
    than the light it hushed.

Pockets of unsteady light.
        The bone—
      the seed
    inside the bone—

          the echo
      and its echo
      and its shape.

    I am resigned.

Can you wash me without my body
Coming apart in your hands?

Call it *wound*—
call it *beginning*—

The bird's beak twisted
into a small circle of awe.

You called it cutting apart,
I called it song.

MADISON JOHNSON

Actually, Yes, Everything is About Race

especially this episode of food network's *chopped* / obviously
/ I am rooting for the token / the black woman / the black
dude from Baltimore / the tiny brown vegan woman even
tho all her food look kinda nasty / over all of these white
boys always / today I am shouting on my sofa for Chef Evelyn
/ because Chef Evelyn says soul food / and she don't mean
what white people search for on yelp / or in my scalp / or in
what used to be jackie n'em old neighborhood/ she means the
food of her soul / she means this is how my grandmamma ate
/ and many a grandmamma before her / in the background,
some white guy says *sriracha* and it sounds like a hate crime
/ the white guys are always saying *sriracha* / always making
reductions / are always sure that they'll win / and I mean sure
/ everyone says it / but they actually mean it / always look at
their dish on the chopping block like they're waiting for it to
hocus pocus into someone else's / like they're used to their
failures hocus pocusing into someone else's / or someone
else / like they want to leap over the judge's table and choke
someone out / and sometimes they do / win / but today /
everyone knows Chef Evelyn's English muffin burger was
bomb / even Chef Eli / who has a pony tail and a surprised
shrug and says / *I guess Evelyn is not just some short twenty-
four-year old / girl / you can write off* / and she kicks his ass /
she apologizes all the way to the finish line / and of course
it's about this / you can learn so much about race in a half
hour cooking show / like how the judges tell Evelyn her ice
cream isn't sweet enough and she says sorry / like how the

judges tell Eli his dessert was straight garbage and he says *well you can't expect me to make a dessert with those ingredients anyway* / like that's not the fucking point of the show / like how the white boy will always blame test / like how the black girl will always cook herself down into an apology / like how the white boy is never sorry for anything / like how the other day I burned my arm getting mac n' cheese out of the oven and it was the closest I have ever felt to black women / glory be a face that looks like mine on tv for a good reason / glory be a woman who reminds me of the spirits in my stomach lining / glory be a warm meal with no reductions and I will always root for the brown chef / and I will never buy the white sob story / because the brown chef don't need sob story / because what is the diasporic kitchen if not one bellowing sob / because the brown chef's sob story is the white chef / is the white man's fork / always in their curry / always in their hair / always breaking down their front door / always scraping the bottom of the plate / asking for more

Preference

tallsuccessfulmasculine35yearsolditalianspanishmixiw

orkout4-6xs/weekyoushouldtoolikequietdinnersandtv

onthecouchasmuchasallnightclubbingmostlytopbutver

satileifyouremanenoughwinkyoushouldbeemployedan

dhavesomegoalsknowyourwayaroundagymcleanandint

endtostaythatwaysonodrugs420andcocktailsandwinew

ithdinnerokicangetkinkybutnothingtoooutrageousnoas

iansblacksfemmesfatsdiseasenooffensejustmypreferen

cebeintelligentandseriouslookingforrealconnectionand

hopefullymore

On the plane, I get so much ass

rubbed on me. My shoulder
shoulders the brief weight
of the attendant's hips,
all the men's packages a cock undiesel
down this aisle, walkers lean right
and this is not political.
The ones by the window,
the ones in the middle,
apologize for their bladders,
ask to be freed from the row—
I'm startled by their perfected womanhood.
That obedience to being small when filled to capacity—
passive polite to remove me from this C,
and I open like a door: in single-ladies file,
the mother of two and woman two-nips-turvy,
shuffle on tiptoes, sucking in their butts and cups.

TOMMY PICO

EXCERPT FROM Food

Keep the dry and wet ingredients in separate bowls before mixing.

You do the egg/cream thing, and I'll take care of the salt/
flower/sugar situation.

Reader, do you hear the moaning plane overhead? Feel the
beating noon heat on yr t-zone?
See the sizzle of foam on the salt water? Poems light up corridors
of the mind, like food. If I owe
poetry to cooking, this is an inheritance of that lineage

I grew up on a food desert, a speck of dust on the map of the
United States—an Indian
reservation east of San Diego in a valley surrounded by
mountains that slice thru the clouds like
a loaf, where the average age of death is 40.7 years old. I am 32.
I live in the busiest city in
America. I am about to eat an orange.

Every feed owes itself to death. Poetry is feed
to the horses
within me.

CARL PHILLIPS

Dominion

Sometimes I take the leather hood off—I
refuse to wear it. As if I were king. Or a man
who's free. Ravens, red-tailed hawks, the usual
flocks of drifting-most-of-the-time strangers
settle the way even things that drift

                                have to, and
I don't care. All over again, I know things that
nobody knows, or wants to—things that, though
prettier, maybe, against the snow

                           of memory, can
still hurt, all the same. Any blame falling where
it falls—that random. That moment each day
when the light traveling across what's always been
mine to at any point take back, or give elsewhere,
becomes just the light again, turning back to dark,
when the branches

                     stir as they've stirred forever,
more tenderly over some of us than others. Sing,
or don't sing. Help me take this leather hood off—
I refuse to wear it. I'm the king. I'm free.

Raise Her Dark Matter

Come witness my cunt
made of deer meat

my drying
dry throat. Men

motorcycle by
the lakeside & behold

I glide as gravel
to the shore,

issue a magic trick.
I raise my dark matter

to the height of kites
cooly strung about

the sky, lie
my stone back

to the rough island.
A fiddle whine

or whistle
interrupts my sun-

spanked day.
This new shadow

above me is the sweat-
salted face

of someone's child—
boy or girl

it doesn't matter.
I curse and

it bursts into doves.

Sunday Morning

after washing,
i slip oil through
my damp braids,
sighing
as the oil
slicks
down
my scalp,
ribbons of
liquid angels
granting me
their honey.

i say to them,
i have a crush
on a girl
named sam.
i imagine
kissing her
with a fistful
of curls
in front of my
bathroom mirror,
in the spot
catching
the most light.
i imagine
this is how
a baby first

learns reverence,
upon finding
all the color
in the world
can fit into
its palm.

i imagine
holding a girl
named sam
& this
makes me
a woman who
defies logic,
gives in
to herself;
& what kind
of daughter
remembers
to want?

i imagine loving
a girl named sam
as oil lifts
the ache
from my head
after the wash;
easy, clean,
as falling
into myself:
a gracious
& simple
anointment.

MEREDITH TALUSAN

DataLounge - Gay Celebrity Gossip, Gay Politics, Gay News and Pointless Bitchery since 1995.

Meredith is not attractive in the slightest. Why does she look like that? She would scare small children.

All the concepts he holds so dearly in his little albino head are nothing but sand castles…completely wiped out when the tide (or logic) rolls in.

This person makes Rachel Dolezal look sane and reasonable by comparison. Also, if you have albinism you are not, by definition, a person of color. If this tedious pigment-less biological male can insist he's a black woman and expect the world to accept that…I don't even know what to say.

I don't understand how this Meredith Trans chick gets all these opportunities to have articles published when (s)he was a stalker / harasser / sociopath?!?!

Albino Black Trans privilege

Why are we discussing trannies here? This is a gay board and trannies are not one of us. I sympathize with injustice, but I object to having them made a topic of soulful blabber.

I have a tranny friend and he's not the least bit whiney about loosing his vagina. He had his corrective surgery and became one of the boys. The reverse story for guys becoming girls never seems to be a happy one.

What did this one do with its genitalia?

What is wrong with its appearance? Is it some kind of albino?

Ew, what is it! Kill it! KILL IT!

Do women who become men ever behave this badly? I never seem to hear about it.

This Talusan sounds like a real little shit. And, regardless of whatever her gender identity might be, she is a biological male behaving in a threatening way to a woman.

Oh c'mon, the poor deluded dear is an albino Filipina tranny, and not easy on the eyes either. Do you really doubt she's had a hard life? Focus your hate on the smug Philly 3 Gay-Bashers rather than this one-tranny army for social justice.

She's fugly, wonder if she's ever had sex.

Filipino lady boys, trannies, etc are always 100% unhinged.

She's acting like a dude trying to force his way onto everyone else.

As a man who prefers transgirls, got something to say, that transgirl is one ugly bitch but if she got a got ass and mouth then why not. Not that I would be in a relationship with an ugly transgirl like that but get all the pleasure out of it and move on to the next pretty transgirl to be with.

MTF trannies tend to be more looney than a Bugs Bunny cartoon, but the Asians bring things to a whole other level.

Leaving aside the exhibitionism, hysteric, delusional, self-absorbed and the host of other tendencies trannies often bring to the table, the Filipino trannies like their women seem to be universally known for exploitation of men.

Forget pronouns—Meredith is so sensitive she might claim a split infinitive as violence against trans women of color.

This Meredith creature must really hate itself. Not only is it a tranny, but also does the skin whitening creams so popular with Asian women and Michael Jackson.

Its obvious that this bucket of Tranny Crazy is looking for pain EVERYWHERE. He finds drama and a reason to play the victim in all situations. It's all about ME ME ME and he will twist any situation to a reason to scream oppression. He is an absolute nightmare and a perfect example of why people are quick to dismiss the Transgender community.

maybe THAT'S why people transition…so they can be a victim.

This guy is fucking delusional. Why he thinks he could possibly pass as a woman is beyond me. His skin bleaching just adds to the hilarity.

Does Meredith still have her cock?

I hope she didn't cut it off. Or, split it down the middle into a makeshift vagina.

One of the few ways MTFs can support themselves after 40 is from generous cockhungry tranny chasers.

I would guess Meredith's story will end very unhappily, especially since she cannot stay on at Cornell forever. What is Meredith going to do with her life when she finally gets her Ph.D.? It's hard to imagine what kind of universities or corporations would put up with her constant drama and nonsense. No wonder she's dragging her heels at getting the hell out of Ithaca.

In a few years, meredith will have been kicked out of Cornell for not graduating, and she will be doing performance art pieces in Williamsburg which will involve her dumping chocolate sauce over her head and screaming, "TRANSPHOBIA! PATRIARCHY! HATE!"

BETH BRANT

Ride the Turtle's Back

A woman grows hard and skinny.
She squeezes into small corners.
Her quick eyes uncover dust and cobwebs.
She reaches out
for flint and sparks fly in the air.
Flames turned loose on fields
burn down to bare seeds
we planted deep.

The corn is white and sweet.
Under its pale, perfect kernels
a rotting cob is betrayal.
It lies in our bloated stomachs.

I lie in Grandmother's bed
and dream the earth into a turtle.
She carries us slowly across the universe.
The sun warms us.
At night the stars do tricks.
The moon caresses us.

We are listening for the sounds of food.

Mother is giving birth, Grandmother says.
Corn whispers.
The earth groans with labor
turning corn yellow in the sun.

I lie in Grandmother's bed.

We listen.

KA'IMILANI LEOTA-SELLERS

When Lillian Posts Pictures of Food on Facebook, I Tell Her She Makes Me Hungry

What I really want comes free from the sea,
gathered from the land, pulled from the roots
with paring knives in hand,
buckets full, fish scales and hoses,
strains of ukulele music playing
in outdoor kitchens, in garages,
Mauna Loa sloping into clouds,
and the tide washing out,
fishermen and divers ready to go,
graduation food, Hawaiian style:

1. Coconut Lu'au, He'e and Tako, suckered tentacles
   soaked in sauce, chewy and sweet
2. Opihi picked fresh from dangerous rocks succulent
   undersides ready to be swallowed quickly with tongue
   and throat
3. Strands of Limu gathered from the ocean's edge, like fine
   hair, soft, iridescent with sand and salt
4. Purple Sweet Potato, with vines that once trailed across
   your yard, now trailing across your tongue, rich, smooth,
   dark on wet lips
5. Poi, my first food, sticky pink, purple-grey, two fingers
   reach deep, eaten with Lomi Salmon, catch the drip,
   swirl, lick, suck, second dipping
6. Lau Lau wrapped tightly with Ti Leaf, steamed and tied
   with string

7. Kalo, the root, the plant, the leaf, the generations of ancestors, and children to come
8. Fresh Pig fed on fern roots in Koa forests, offered to the earth, fire, black stones, imu, buried, transcended
9. Poke, Crab Legs, Sashimi, gleaming, translucent Fried Fish, all those fish that the neighbor boy could name when he was five: Menpache, Ta'ape, Ahi, Aha, Weke, Palani, Ono, Kole, Ulua, Uhu, Moi, glazed eyes white, fins crispy, watch out for small bones
10. And then, the extras, Charsiu, Portuguese Bean Soup, Pork and Peas, Potato Salad, fresh, hot rice, the kind that sticks to everything, powdered mochi, pink, red, and green, and all those little Filipino desserts wrapped in coconut leaves...

I drool, I dream, I remember,
my stomach aching for what it can't have,
the hamburger curling in my stomach lurches,
the french-fries coil round my intestines,
make me sick, make me home-
sick for food.

American Wedding

In america,
I place my ring
on your cock
where it belongs.
No horsemen
bearing terror,
no soldiers of doom
will swoop in
and sweep us apart.
They're too busy
looting the land
to watch us.
They don't know
we need each other
critically.
They expect us to call in sick,
watch television all night,
die by our own hands.
They don't know
we are becoming powerful.
Every time we kiss
we confirm the new world coming.

What the rose whispers
before blooming
I vow to you.
I give you my heart,

a safe house.
I give you promises other than
milk, honey, liberty.
I assume you will always
be a free man with a dream.
In america,
place your ring
on my cock
where it belongs.
Long may we live
to free this dream.

DEMIAN DINÉYAZHI'

Untitled (For Andrea Smith)

R.I.S.E.: *Radical Indigenous Survivance & Empowerment*

if one were to develop
A FEMINIST history centering
NATIVE WOMEN,
feminist history in this
COUNTRY
would start in 1492
with the R E S I S T A N C E
to patriarchal
C O L O N I Z A T I O N .

IRENE VILLASEÑOR

10 Truths and a Lie

I'm prepared for the next race riot /
Can't tell you exactly how I was trained
(though) /
Elders encouraged me to stay safe /
by maintaining secret identities
(yet) /
When we want to see ourselves, /
we visit anthropological exhibits /
It's trendy to exoticize someone like me
now (again) /
I keep getting mistaken for a stripper /
So little is expected of me /
that my accomplishments are subversive
(really) /
I'm the next generation after a tragedy /
after an atrocity /
after a genocide /
Being invisible may prolong my survival
(but) /
My truths are more powerful than their fictions.

CAMERON AWKWARD-RICH

The Cure for What Ails You

is a good run. At least, according to my mother
which has seemed, all my life, like cruelty —

when I had a fever, for example, or a heart,
shipwrecked & taking on the flood. But now,

of course, this is what I tell my friend whose eye
has been twitching since last Tuesday, what I

tell my student who can't seem to focus
her arguments, who believes, still,

that it's possible to save the world
in 10-12 pages, double-spaced & without irony

I'm asking *Have you tried going for a run?*
You know, to clear your head? this mother-voice

drowning out what I once thought
to be my own. I'll admit that when that man

became the president, before terrified I felt
relief — finally, here was the bald face

of the country & now everyone had to look
at it. Everyone had to see what my loves

for their lives, could not unsee. Cruelty
after all is made of distance —

sign here & the world ends
somewhere else. The world. The literal

world. I hold my face close to the blue
light of the screen until my head aches.

Until I'm sick & like a child I just want
someone to touch me with cool hands

& say *yes, you're right, something is wrong*
stay here in bed until the pain stops & Oh

mother, remember the night
when, convinced that you were dying,

you raced to the hospital clutching
your heart & by the time you arrived

you were fine. You were sharp
as a blade. Five miles in & I can't stop

thinking about that video. There's a man
with his arms raised

in surrender. He was driving
his car. His own car & they're charging him

bellowing like bulls *I didn't shoot you, motherfucker,*
you should feel lucky for that. Yes. Ok.

Fine. My body too can be drawn
like any weapon.

EDUARDO MARTINEZ-LEYVA

I Never Wanted to Speak

of the house facing Cowboy Park
where my childhood pets are buried.

Eight small skulls scattered, each
a burned-out bulb keeping the fig tree

company, guarding the needles
I'd eventually unearth. My neighbor,

the infected queen, taught me
how to shoot down pigeons.

Think of them as compliments, he'd say.
By the time I was old enough to know

what he meant, it was too late
for him. Still, he slept inside me

for many seasons, cocking
his shotgun at a flinching sky.

Disguised in pill and sneer,
he waited for warmth to enter the body.

MONICA HAND

Things that stink

Drunks
their breath their sweat
especially when they are lying on top of you
or when they have fallen off of you and you are listening to
    them snore and fart
when they are your father stumbling up the stairs or passed
    out on the sofa
in all his clothes smelling of cigarettes vomit and stale
    women's cologne
when he is smacking your mother around and you can smell
    her near
you are supposed to be sleeping
when they sit next to you on the subway
when they yell "hey baby" as you are walking to school
when they are happy dancing with their pants falling off
slobbering on your neck playing cards talking shit
just mean

when they are lilies at a funeral

bed sheets the day after when the dark has removed its mask

I Have A Time Machine

But unfortunately it can only travel into the future
at a rate of one second per second,

which seems slow to the physicists and to the grant
committees and even to me.

But I manage to get there, time after time, to the next
moment and to the next.

Thing is, I can't turn it off. I keep zipping ahead—
well, not *zipping*—And if I try

to get out of this time machine, open the latch,
I'll fall into space, unconscious,

then desiccated! And I'm pretty sure I'm afraid of that.
So I stay inside.

There's a window, though. It shows the past.
It's like a television or fish tank

but it's never live, it's always over. The fish swim
in backward circles.

Sometimes it's like a rearview mirror, another chance
to see what I'm leaving behind,

and sometimes like blackout, all that time
wasted sleeping.

Myself age eight, whole head burnt with embarrassment
at having lost a library book.

Myself lurking in a candled corner expecting
to be found charming.

Me holding a rose though I want to put it down
so I can smoke.

Me exploding at my mother who explodes at me
because the explosion

of some dark star all the way back struck hard
at mother's mother's mother.

I turn away from the window, anticipating a blow.
I thought I'd find myself

an old woman by now, travelling so light in time.
But I haven't gotten far at all.

Strange not to be able to pick up the pace as I'd like;
the past is so horribly fast.

QWO-LI DRISKILL

Open Letter to Ian Birk, Seattle Police Officer who Shot John T. Williams on August 20, 2010

Dear Ian
> I can't believe
> you killed
> my friend

Warning

Negroes,
Sweet and docile,
Meek, humble and kind:
Beware the day
They change their mind!
Wind
In the cotton fields,
Gentle Breeze:
Beware the hour
It uproots trees!

A Boy with Baleen for Teeth

My father wished
            to cast me back-
wards caste and all:
            a wrong catch,
swaddled in dreams,
            saffron amniotic
dripping off my black
            whalebone gown.

. . .

My baleen burst through
pursed lips. When I smiled

Sunday's Lutherans gasped
then laughed to hide

horror with *he will outgrow it.*
I opened my jaws

and sucked the plank-
ton from their eyes.

. . .

My father's pliers gripped
            my plates and he etched
the story of the son he wanted

onto my keratin. I gouged it out
and into the channels smeared
India ink and plunged, a fallen

star into the abyss.

. . .

What to make
of deep silence
that swallows the body,

crushing brown boys
with its tongue—
what a fool I was,

drawn to any
glimmer. A whaler
tore my dress

then stuck me
with his harpoon
after we kissed

in a haze of chanteys
and Cutty Sark.
I wanted to taste

any body
that shines in the dark.

. . .

Night pulsed from the clouds
in nested song and I was rain too,

starved for seasons, breaching
at dusk: a silhouette

on a darker sea—
for seasons I was faceless

trying to swallow constellations,
to roll a star-map on my tongue.

. . .

Once when lunging
                    into the moon the sea
showed me my face
                    as I trembled midair.
Stars shone through
                    the holes of my body.

Untitled (Destroying Flesh)

UNIVERSAL CROP TOPS FOR ALL THE SELF-CANONIZED SAINTS OF
BECOMING. PRIMAL SELF-RECOGNITION DISASSEMBLES AS/IT FORMS,
TRANSFERRING CORPORAL MATTER INTO THE VIRTUAL AND IT
DOUBLES BACK AS A FANTASY OF OURSELVES... OR PERHAPS ITS ALL
JUST A NIGHTMARE. LIKE THAT TIME I REALIZED THAT FOR US BY US
WAS A MESSAGE MORE SEDUCTIVE TO THEM THAN IT EVER WAS TO US.
NOT THAT US IS EVEN US AT THIS POINT, AS THE SEPARATIONS
BETWEEN DISSOLVE WITH EVERY CAUSTIC 'AGREE TO TERMS OF
SERVICE.' THERE ARE SO MANY SKELETAL REMAINS IN LOCKED
XANGAS LIVEJOURNAL AND MYSPACE ACCOUNTS. THE FINAL
FRONTIER OF THE OLD TRIBES AND THEOLOGIES. WHEN HOT TOPIC
AND GAP WERE HOT TOPIC AND GAP. THE CULT OF PREDETERMINED
VOLITION IS DEAD—THE SACRILEGE OF THE
OLD-ENOUGH-TO-NOT-BE-NEW AND EXPANSIVE DIGITAL FRONTIER
CONSUMED ALL THE WIGGERS, GOTH GIRLS, PUNKS AND YUPPIES OF
OLD, SERVING A GENERATION OF SELF CREATED DEITIES, HALLOWED
BY VIRTUE OF THE SINGULARITY AND BREADTH OF THE ICONOCLASM
AS THEY ARE FORCED TO REGIFURE THE SOCIAL.

THE OSTENSIBLY LOST BOYS GIRLS AND OTHERWISE WHO CRUCIFY THE
ALWAYS-ALREADY-DEAD VERSION OF THEMSELVES CURRENTLY
UNABLE TO CHOOSE WHICH SONG TO PLAY-TO-ITS-END ON THE WAY
FROM START TO FINAL TRAIN STOP AND OPT FOR A 40 MINUTE MIX
THAT MUTES THE BOUNDARIES THAT PASSIVE-AGGRESSIVELY FRAME
EVERY DECISION BETWEEN DUNK/BOOT, NATURAL/MAYBELLINE,
CHEST BINDER OR BRA, TUCK OR GET-STUCK-GETTING-CLOCKED.

THE RELIGIOUS AND COMPULSIVE NEED && PRAYER FOR DURATION
PERMEANCE AND PERMANENCE IN SOUND IS ANSWERED BY THE
ADVENT OF THE MIX OVER SONG. THE SUBLIME AND RAPTUROUS
POWER OF THE HYMN TO BREAK YOLKS GIVEN AS THE PERFECT
PASTICHE OR LAYERING THAT ALLOWS US FOR A MOMENT TO ESCAPE
GENRE, THE 5-OR-SO MINUTE LIMIT OF SONGS PROPER AND THE
UNIT-CUBES WE FIND OURSELVES ATOMIZED IN DIVIDED BY A
SURFACE MADE OF CLICKS SHARING REPRESENTATIVE DATA FILES,
EACH ONE DESTROYING OUR FLESH AS IT FADES INTO NOUMENON.

Black Sonnet

A black child lies in blood and I'm still black.
I scan news on my phone and I'm still black.
They call my name to board and I'm still black.
I sit and sip a Sprite and I'm still black.
We take off right on time and I'm still black.
I peer at vast blue sea and I'm still black.
I take my black tea black and I'm still black.
I read a piece by Marx and I'm still black.
I get lost and turn back and I'm still black.
I make the right slight right and I'm still black.
I ring the front bell twice and I'm still black.
My love smiles with her eyes and I'm still black.
We kick it for a bit and I'm still black.
I turn off all the lights and I'm still black.

Wet Dream

it's embarrassing, how bad I want you
how wet I am, like you could drown in me.

you spread my legs & slip a finger inside me
then two / an arm / a torso
until you've disappeared, a casualty
of my greedy body.

I'm ashamed of how much water
my body holds. I'm more ocean
than girl
but you'll take what you can get

cuz everything my pussy touches
turns to gold.

I cum like a goddamn tsunami & next thing you know
experts are calling my orgasm a natural disaster
& you're collecting checks
from FEMA.

so it goes.

I'm ashamed of how much water
my body holds. I sit on your face
& you cough up water like a drowned man
washed up on shore.

sometimes, I just wanna ride you into the sunset
like in the movies.

is that too much to ask?

Erasure of Girlhood

I walk behind my   & he tells me it's like our first &   fear swell
in my chest like a wet storm that   forecaster would ever wish   predict
tracks left oil   after   he put the fire out & now   in search
        & he asks me   down & I whine   far from the river
    into January   cold & coyotes out here &   down &
down & my   numbs from the cold &   my face &   bury my teeth
            without fleeing & the   seared my   rose in my
    & the sap from the tree   into the air & the stink of it smeared my
& the river came back   I could always hold the longest underwater
  I lie   my pants   pulled   tongue
        pain   hips   bile   throat
cut down bled into   a flood of salt   my breath whine
        now lovers always stare into   kiss my breath, I
never   to the mattress

She Calls Once That Is A Lie

When she calls in the morning
I've changed my number address identifying features
I've sacrificed my name when she calls in the morning
With news she's selling my teeth on eBay
The teeth she broke off
One by one
While I was sleeping that is a lie when she
Calls in the morning I was awake
Each time she whittled away my ability to bite
Once on VH1 in a thrash metal rockumentary that is a lie
It was at the Kentucky Derby when she calls in the morning
She's taken all my hats and next my hair
And my scalp is an angry red gash
Once eating toffee by the sea that is a lie
When she calls in the morning it was a rest-stop
In Jersey and the assortment was unreal
And of all things I chose Dentine
Once I knew all the lemon drops by names
And identifying features they had names
When she calls in the morning she wants the children
When she calls in the morning and then the house
And the hospital where they won't operate on me
There are no spare parts not even a space between
Whistling
Like a fist of the bank in wet
Season lying through her teeth

Elegy for the Living and Breathing

Photographs of people under water make me breathe
    deeper. And sometimes the people aren't

people, but holy embodiments of Atlantic trauma.
    Anything with a face submerged

or squalling vengeance. To be brought down to my
    misery, to silence my anxiety, I gulp into

my lungs' pockets for a few cents of oxygen. Can
    you believe we still have to ask nicely?

Can you believe some of us still drown in our own
    lungs? Today it was a picture of Muhammed

Ali boxing underwater, and because he can no longer
    hold his own breath, I rattle the coins in my

chest. Even exhaling, there is audacity in my lungs.
    We are in need of a plan. Let's meet

somewhere between my sternum and the equator for
    survival lessons. Let's deflate something

that we can all agree is monstrous, and take its air
    inside us. Let's witness an infant kicking

and grabbing through a pool. For those moments she
  believes herself back in utero. The compulsion

within someone who wants only to make it to
  the other side on a single clutch of air.

Paisahood

Is this what it means to be a Paisa
      Hearing Mariachi tune instruments
      to play out my eleventh hour
      Too tired from migrant labor
      to ask the sun why this is so
      Hoping Ama y Apa are all right
      Counting almond rows and out-singing the tractor
      to pass the time.

Is this what it means to be a Paisa
      To be visited by the corn-sent saint
      jugs full of water hanging from both hands
      plaid shirt unbuttoned just enough
      tip of a serpentine tattoo visible
      me wanting nothing more than to follow it
      to canonization

      to Paisahood.

The Body in August

Because when I was a child, God would pull me up into Her lap. Because
when She pulled me up into Her lap, She would read to me. Because the
story She read most was the one I liked least. Because every day She'd open
that thin green book and say, This is the story of your life. Because, from
beginning to end, there were only three pages.

I believe in that road that is infinite and black and goes on blindly forever. I
believe crocodiles swallow rocks to help them digest crab. Because up until
the twentieth century, people could still die from sensation. And because
my hunger is so deep, I am ashamed to lift my head.

Because memory—not gravity—pins us to this trembling. And when God
first laid eyes on us, She went mad from envy. Because if the planet had a
back door, we'd all still be there—waiting for the air to approve our entry.
Because your eyes were the only time the peonies said yes to me. Because
no matter how many times I died, I always woke up again—happy.

Then, last night, after I'd yelled at him for the first time, my new son
dreamt we went walking inside the trees. When we came across a squirrel,
he said, I'd kicked it. Then the squirrel changed into a thin green book,
which we read.

Because when God became a small child, I pulled Her up into my lap.
Because when I pulled Her into my lap—to please Her—I opened my
blouse. Because Her mouth is an impossibly pink place, a gaping raw
cathedral, which She opened, teeth-to-nipple, then clamped down.

Maskot #1: "They sure do love them some black pain."

Tell us duh one bout dem chirren and duh bullets dey eat

Tell us duh one bout dem roaches makin love to yo feet

Tell us duh one bout yo grandmammy's hands:
    callused and cookin, cansuh everywhere but her hands
Tell us bout her mouf too: "Oh Lawdy Jesus" "Wrench around…"
    "Bout scared me half to DEATH" she make purty sounds

Tell us duh one bout white people cuttin you
    in line [did yuh neck do that back
and forf thing finguh waggin
    lips lippin "nuh uh no she di-int"]

Tell us duh one bout duh woman duh rope and duh bridge
    [O dere was a baby dat fell out and bumped its head
    on duh waduh followin duh drinkin gourd
or nah?]

Is you submittin to my journal or nah?
You spoken word or nah?
You hopin whitey gets his just due
flippin duh bird or nah?

Savage poem, aggressive and shit, beastly comeuppance
    all da boys in duh hinterland dead
    cause uh duh hoodie monster

You gots anymo uh dem po-lice poems wit duh
Hippity Hop refrences wit dem thugs and da trees?
I sho love me some Hippity Hop refrences
But why thugs always smokin on dem trees
Don't dey know dey histry is
to run from burnin trees?

Duh way you write nigga makes me thank [of] my mama

Tell us duh one bout music comin from duh eyes
Was dat "Purple Rain" or "Duh Coluh Purple" or is it a suhprise?
Tell us "stolen milk," "watch my chirren when I'm gone,"
    "Don't let him see me dis way," "I'm so glad Jesus is my home!"

Got anymo uh dem poems bout Celie?
Got some "Give us us free"
in yo packet, yo pote-folio, or yo spahklin CV?

How much fo duh WIC-EBT-lost-bus-card sonnet?
How much fo slave wenches wearin waduh-melons as bonnets?

What you got up in dat verse what you got up in dat verse
    [a couple uh guns/ a couple uh blunts/ a couple uh suicide
    doors/ Dior chokers/ all duh shit you adore?]

Dat one gets me so hard/wet at night in duh dahk

Duh dahk got a poem too soundin jus like a knife
    slidin through some cone-bread

Soft as a baby

Tell us duh one again bout duh baby

Ghazal After Quebec City

Childhood:
A mosque is a home
Clear laughter lilting through corridors bright eyes
    glimmering in lazy sunlight
My hands are always warmer inside and the imam's words feel
    like water on my skin
Aaj jaane ki zid na kaaro (do not go gentle into that cold
    french night)

Migration:
The first time someone called me a terrorist
My knees shook legs
I was ten years old and it was winter in New Brunswick
The second time someone called me a terrorist
My face burned
I was eleven years old and it was summer in Alberta
The third time:
I broke his nose.

Listen:
Ma told me that some people are softer than others
And some people are knives.

Imagine:
You are bowing your head down before your creator (your
    heart is light)
Your son has the brownest eyes you have known (he reminds
    you of your father)

And then there is a bullet in your back (prayer is like rain and
  your soul is ripe)

Do not look away:
Alexandre Bissonnette screamed Allah Akbar
Before he [slaughtered] my brothers and sisters (please go
  gently into that dark night)
A knife in a house full of flowers
Shhh there is a time and place for everything but right now I
  find it hard to exist.

And now:
I may not be a believer
Might in fact be quite a sinner (dope slinger microphone
  slicker)
But Rumi told me to drink the wine that moves my soul
To become lost in the call (look for the light)
So I take the 1c bus to the old mosque in West Windsor
And let myself fall into the brightness (there is always light).

GEORGE ABRAHAM

EXCERPT FROM Inheritance

I. Textbook Fragments

[DNA TEST: IF YOU DRAW BLOOD / FROM A PALESTINIAN, BOIL / IT'S SUBSTANCE UNTIL / IT IS A TREMBLING WHITE[1] / BODY OF UNZIPPING / HELIX & DANCING VINE / PRACTICALLY AN ERASURE / OF ITSELF, THERE IS A ONE-IN-THREE CHANCE / THIS BODY SHARES / A CHROMOSOME WITH THE OPPRESSOR .[2]]

[FOOTNOTE: DO NOT CALL THIS WAR / GENOCIDE BUT INSTEAD, ETHNIC CLEANSING / PALESTINIANS NEED NOT LOOK AT / THE RACIALIZATION / OF IT ALL. THIS ENCOURAGES THE OPPRESSOR'S / POWER COMPLEX. MOST PEOPLE / IN THE MIDDLE EAST ARE WHITE / ANYWAYS[3] WHAT IS NARRATIVE IF NOT THE BLOOD / IT CARRIES?

---

1 Whereas, the oppressor implants their DESIGN
into every h(a)unted bloodline—
this country: everyone's
inheritance.

2 By which you mean, the oppressor
runs through the bodies
their bullets miss?

3 By virtue of expulsion
or white phosphorus?
i.e. choose your   .

WHAT ARE YOU IF NOT THE TRAUMA YOU INHERIT? [4]]

[FACT: STATISTICALLY SPEAKING, PALESTINIANS ARE THE POPULATION WITH THE HIGHEST PERCENTAGE OF PHDS IN THE WORLD. [5]]

[~~ISN'T THIS BIOLOGY THE MOST OPPRESSIVE THING YOUR MOTHER GIFTED YOU~~]

II. Family History Fragments—a reverse chronology

israeli man asks me to tie him up and fuck him. says he has a POWER COMPLEX.

after taking a sex hiatus, i contract mono. why does my BIOLOGY fail me?

the first panic attack in college felt like a heart attack. ER tech says i just need sleep.

(~~the first time i was raped i was outside myself~~)

---

4   Every time i open
    my mouth: a chorus
    of BLOOD.

    i think of it as history.

    the oppressor calls it
    DIVERSITY or NARRATIVE
    hence FABLE.

5   & look at how far that's gotten us.

my parents fear college is making an ACTIVIST of me.
what happened to our son?
why don't you come home anymore?

i eat hummus too, we're practically the same: SOLIDARITY.

third grade: *you're dirty because you're Ay-rab.*
same year—baba almost dies of a heart attack.

age 6: i ask mama why we never visit palestine. why we never come home anymore.

my parents decide not to teach me arabic growing up: DEFENSE MECHANISM. or maybe i was never *theirs*.

teta dies of cancer before i am old enough to understand. grape leaves blossom in her garden, little hands reaching for some invisible heaven. like her BIOLOGY escaped her—

baba takes over shop at age 20 after sido dies of a heart attack. his mother, widowed in this country where no one speaks her language.

sido is forced out of his home at age 20. hence, mama is born in america. hence i am *american*.

settlement camps surround Ramallah, make an eviction notice of teta's house: cell MIGRATION. fatal OVERGROWTH.

auntie used to say the settlers took the hilltops & aquifers first. uprooted the olive trees & waged BIOLOGICAL WARFARE against our lineage: reclamation. of INHERITANCE.

(~~or was it GENOCIDE?~~)

when the colonizers emptied the villages, they lined up the
men to be executed in front of their families, raped the women
& planted pine trees over the wreckage. they were miles away
from my teta's town. just far enough so no one could hear the
screams.

even when the land was ours
it wasn't.

(~~this is how i feel about my body sometimes~~)

III. self-portrait as unidentified Palestinian Village, post-Nakba

what the textbooks fail to mention:
i was whole once. this flesh
wasn't always the site of a bloodied
ecosystem; these rose-soaked
kuffiyat—a thousand dancing ghosts.

i was not always crumbled
fortress & concrete
partition. once, the bodies
in me could sing
without screaming—

i have never known
this   .

trees singing different nation's
wind-song; roots grasping buried

kin like only a mother could; even
when the colonizers plant life
in me, they make amnesia
of my childrens' laughter
& call my hollow, false
witness. the question
marks in your history books?
i am an erasure

of myself? my BIOLOGY
fails me? i mean to say,
once i had a body
to choke on.

Abuela Dice Que Spilled Salt Goes
Over the Shoulder

Por que no tenemos una pais anymore
cuando we lived in Santo Domingo
we watched Trujillo spill 100 daughters
onto the street y lo sigue de este
recuerdas the memory of a city
turns you to salt   esta de Dios
this would have been your fatherland
before men who were fathers
took it apart   con sus manos sucios
por supuesto   nos decidio
we had to wash ourselves of home
in order to survive   we flew
so that su madre might be untouched
sacrificio para sacrificio
sangre por sangre
what else could we have done but taken
the house spilling into bricks in front of us
and sprinkle it into the ocean?
el oceano no hay azucar
salt is always hungry
salt is what made the men forget
their country had a name
that was not the name of a man
who gave every mirror his name
mijo   la sal esta pequena pero
the ocean will never hold your face
so kindly   y este is how men grow vain
and forget to wash the blood
from their hands before they hug their daughters

NIKKI GIOVANNI

My First Memory (of Librarians)

This is my first memory:
A big room with heavy wooden tables that sat on a creaky
    wood floor
A line of green shades—bankers' lights—down the center
Heavy oak chairs that were too low or maybe I was simply
    too short
        For me to sit in and read
So my first book was always big

In the foyer up four steps a semi-circle desk presided
To the left side the card catalogue
On the right newspapers draped over what looked like
    a quilt rack
Magazines face out from the wall

The welcoming smile of my librarian
The anticipation in my heart
All those books—another world—just waiting
At my fingertips.

When a Nigga Calls You a Faggot

You gotta laugh at least once.
Like the pot calling the kettle
A more dangerous thing.
When he spits in your mouth,
you must swallow the sour,
hurt of anxiety. How your lips
make him salivate.
When he swings his fist,
duck down and tackle him to
the ground with soft kisses.
When a nigga calls you a faggot,
He's calling you by his first name.
He's telling you about his-self.
His own fault lines splitting his tongue,
toxic and tender. He's crying for help
from the bottom of the ocean.
When it discharges from his throat,
imagine it lands on the shores
of which both your bodies washed up.
When a nigga calls you a faggot,
you still gotta call him brother.
You still gotta pray he makes it
home at night.

The Woman Hanging from the Thirteenth Floor Window

She is the woman hanging from the 13th floor
window. Her hands are pressed white against the
concrete moulding of the tenement building. She
hangs from the 13th floor window in east Chicago,
with a swirl of birds over her head. They could
be a halo, or a storm of glass waiting to crush her.

She thinks she will be set free.

The woman hanging from the 13th floor window
on the east side of Chicago is not alone.
She is a woman of children, of the baby, Carlos,
and of Margaret, and of Jimmy who is the oldest.
She is her mother's daughter and her father's son.
She is several pieces between the two husbands
she has had. She is all the women of the apartment
building who stand watching her, watching themselves.

When she was young she ate wild rice on scraped down
plates in warm wood rooms. It was in the farther
north and she was the baby then. They rocked her.

She sees Lake Michigan lapping at the shores of
herself. It is a dizzy hole of water and the rich
live in tall glass houses at the edge of it. In some
places Lake Michigan speaks softly, here, it just sputters

and butts itself against the asphalt. She sees
other buildings just like hers. She sees other
women hanging from many-floored windows
counting their lives in the palms of their hands
and in the palms of their children's hands.

She is the woman hanging from the 13th floor window
on the Indian side of town. Her belly is soft from
her children's births, her worn levis swing down below
her waist, and then her feet, and then her heart.
She is dangling.

The woman hanging from the 13th floor hears voices.
They come to her in the night when the lights have gone
dim. Sometimes they are little cats mewing and scratching
at the door, sometimes they are her grandmother's voice,
and sometimes they are gigantic men of light whispering
to her to get up, to get up, to get up. That's when she wants
to have another child to hold onto in the night, to be able
to fall back into dreams.

And the woman hanging from the 13th floor window
hears other voices. Some of them scream out from below
for her to jump, they would push her over. Others cry softly
from the sidewalks, pull their children up like flowers and gather
them into their arms. They would help her, like themselves.

But she is the woman hanging from the 13th floor window,
and she knows she is hanging by her own fingers, her
own skin, her own thread of indecision.

She thinks of Carlos, of Margaret, of Jimmy.
She thinks of her father, and of her mother.

She thinks of all the women she has been, of all
the men. She thinks of the color of her skin, and
of Chicago streets, and of waterfalls and pines.
She thinks of moonlight nights, and of cool spring storms.
Her mind chatters like neon and northside bars.
She thinks of the 4 a.m. lonelinesses that have folded
her up like death, discordant, without logical and
beautiful conclusion. Her teeth break off at the edges.
She would speak.

The woman hangs from the 13th floor window crying for
the lost beauty of her own life. She sees the
sun falling west over the grey plane of Chicago.
She thinks she remembers listening to her own life
break loose, as she falls from the 13th floor
window on the east side of Chicago, or as she
climbs back up to claim herself again.

JOSEPH O. LEGASPI

Chelsea Piers

My lover and I stroll down the piers,

post pescetarian dinner, in midsummer.

He points to the moon, veiled by clouds.

The Hudson River murmurs soft waves.

Across, the buildings glitter like theater.

Our arms damp, lamps lend themselves

to fantasy of the last two men on earth.

But as I reach for his hand, he pulls it

away, looks hurriedly around. Suddenly

I stand awash in brutal history, periphery

of sanctuary and danger. We are those

punished for our affections. The silent

seagulls disguised as larks. His denial

plunges silver-finned into the river.

transcript of an MTA audition

i sit wide-legged & grab my crotch
i sit wide-legged & adjust my nuts
i sit wide-legged & shift my dick two millimeters to the left
i sit wide-legged & scratch my balls
i sit wide-legged & consider the weight of my nutsack
i sit wide-legged & cup my nutsack
i sit wide-legged & estimate my nutsack weighs about five ounces
i sit wide-legged & hold my dick like a gun
i sit wide-legged & aim my dick at that chick over there
i sit wide-legged & pull the trigger
i sit wide-legged & murder these hoes
i sit wide-legged & smell my trigger finger
i sit wide-legged & slouch & side-eye whoever dares to watch

FRANCISCO ARAGÓN

2012

24th & Mission BART station laundry
hamper wide screen television Dupont
Circle cassette of my sister's voice cassette
of my father's Court House Metro
torn photograph of my grandfather
"Untitled" by Malaquias Montoya smart
phone theater programs my father's
gold watch boxed up photographs lap
top Fair Oaks the Mission Noe Valley
skateboard *Mandorla* the New
Yorker Venus in Fur Sex with Strangers a few
DVDs *Pilgrimage PALABRA* I was a short
skinny boy Midnight in Paris Yuba Poppie
depression *My Vocabulary Did This to Me*

if my slumlord allowed pets

i'd adopt every
after hour paw
mauled in battle

trimmed with scabs
toppling trash
for fries & wing tips

fur splattered
with egg foo young

these streets
weren't paved
for tenderness

a tabby's pregnant belly
low-hanging
as a rain cloud

a swollen nimbus
grazing the ground

FATIMAH ASGHAR

Pluto Shits on the Universe

On February 7, 1979, Pluto crossed over Neptune's orbit and became the eighth planet from the sun for twenty years. A study in 1988 determined that Pluto's path of orbit could never be accurately predicted. Labeled as "chaotic," Pluto was later discredited from planet status in 2006.

Today, I broke your solar system. Oops.
My bad. Your graph said I was supposed
to make a nice little loop around the sun.

Naw.

I chaos like a motherfucker. Ain't no one can
chart me. All the other planets, they think
I'm annoying. They think I'm an escaped
moon, running free.

Fuck your moon. Fuck your solar system.
Fuck your time. Your year? Your year ain't
shit but a day to me. I could spend your
whole year turning the winds in my bed. Thinking
about rings and how Jupiter should just pussy
on up and marry me by now. Your day?

That's an asswipe. A sniffle. Your whole day
is barely the start of my sunset.

My name means hell, bitch. I am hell, bitch. All the cold
you have yet to feel. Chaos like a motherfucker.
And you tried to order me. Called me ninth.
Somewhere in the mess of graphs and math and compass
you tried to make me follow rules. Rules? Fuck your
rules. Neptune, that bitch slow. And I deserve all the sun
I can get, and all the blue-gold sky I want around me.

It is February 7th, 1979 and my skin is more
copper than any sky will ever be. More metal.
Neptune is bitch-sobbing in my rearview,
and I got my running shoes on and all this sky that's all mine.

Fuck your order. Fuck your time. I realigned the cosmos.
I chaosed all the hell you have yet to feel. Now all your kids
in the classrooms, they confused. All their clocks:
wrong. They don't even know what the fuck to do.
They gotta memorize new songs and shit. And the other
planets, I fucked their orbits. I shook the sky. Chaos like
a motherfucker.

It is February 7th, 1979. The sky is blue-gold:
the freedom of possibility.

Today, I broke your solar system. Oops. My bad.

to whom it may concern:

i left my fishnet thigh
high on your carpet.
cherry stems littered
on the bed. cobras in
my chest
i'm messy
borrowed the sun
to warm my feet
left a trail of forest
in your kitchen. used
your toothbrush
to do my baby hair,
molted a skin
on your sofa
i've never
been more
unapologetic
in my life

MARK AGUHAR

LITANIES TO MY HEAVENLY BROWN BODY

FUCK YOUR WHITENESS

FUCK YOUR BEAUTY

FUCK YOUR CHEST HAIR

FUCK YOUR BEARD

FUCK YOUR PRIVILEGE

FUCK THAT YOU AREN'T MADE TO FEEL SHAME ALWAYS

FUCK YOUR THINNESS

FUCK YOUR MUSCLES

FUCK YOUR ATTRACTIVE FATNESS

FUCK YOUR SHAMING ME FOR NOTHING

FUCK YOUR ACCUSATIONS THAT I PRODUCE SHAME

FUCK YOUR READING ME AS A CARICATURE

FUCK YOUR DESTRUCTION OF MY PERSONHOOD

FUCK YOUR MARGINALIZATION OF MY IDENTITY

FUCK YOUR JUDGING ME FOR SELF CARE

FUCK YOUR ABILITY TO BE ASSERTIVE

FUCK YOUR LACK OF SOCIALIZATION TO BE A SUBMISSIVE

FUCK YOUR ASKING ME TO PRODUCE SAFETY FOR YOU AND
    NOT MYSELF

FUCK THE AMOUNT OF EFFORT I EXERT TO GET LESS THAN
    ENOUGH CONSIDERATION

FUCK THAT THE AMOUNT OF SPACE I TAKE UP IN THE WORLD
    IS CONSTANTLY QUESTIONED

FUCK THAT PEOPLE THINK I'M A SLUT

FUCK THAT YOU CAN DEMAND ATTENTION

FUCK THAT I'M WILLING TO GIVE YOU WHAT I CAN'T HAVE

FUCK THAT YOUR VALUES AND YOUR ACTIONS NEVER MATCH

UP WHEN IT COMES TO ME
FUCK THAT I CAN'T EXPECT ANYTHING FROM ANYONE
FUCK THAT THE AMOUNT OF WORK I PUT INTO THE BEAUTY OF
    MY INTELLECT AND MY TALENT IS STILL NEVER ENOUGH

AMEN

BLESSED ARE THE SISSIES
BLESSED ARE THE BOI DYKES
BLESSED ARE THE PEOPLE OF COLOR MY BELOVED KITH AND KIN
BLESSED ARE THE TRANS
BLESSED ARE THE HIGH FEMMES
BLESSED ARE THE SEX WORKERS
BLESSED ARE THE AUTHENTIC
BLESSED ARE THE DIS-IDENTIFIERS
BLESSED ARE THE GENDER ILLUSIONISTS
BLESSED ARE THE NON-NORMATIVE
BLESSED ARE THE GENDERQUEERS
BLESSED ARE THE KINKSTERS
BLESSED ARE THE DISABLED
BLESSED ARE THE HOT FAT GIRLS
BLESSED ARE THE WEIRDO-QUEERS
BLESSED IS THE SPECTRUM
BLESSED IS CONSENT
BLESSED IS RESPECT
BLESSED ARE THE BELOVED WHO I DIDN'T DESCRIBE, I
    COULDN'T DESCRIBE, WILL LEARN TO DESCRIBE AND
    RESPECT AND LOVE

AMEN

I-797C Notice of Action

REQUEST FOR APPLICANT TO APPEAR FOR INITIAL INTERVIEW
APPLICATION NUMBER MSC XXXXXXX058
A# A XXX XXX 961
Notice Date: July 24, 2014
Priority Date: July 24, 2014
Date of Arrival: February 20, 1984

hereby notified to appear
  how often do you have sex
to adjust status
  what color is his toothbrush
his birth certificate
  what side of the bed does he sleep on
resident alien
  how much does he make
your husband must come with you
  what's his mother's name
we may videotape you
  where did you buy your rings
bring an interpreter
  what are his siblings' spouses' names
in a sealed envelope bring
  what's his father's name
failure to appear
  what's *his* father's name
please appear, as scheduled below
  do you love him

supporting evidence
why do you love him
Tuesday, March 17, 2015 8:00am USCIS, Chicago, IL

don't mention citizenship
talk about love, how you got married for love

Catching Copper

My brothers have
a bullet.

They keep their bullet
on a leash shiny
as a whip of blood.

My brothers walk their bullet
with a limp—a clipped
hip bone.

My brothers' bullet
is a math-head, is all geometry,
from a distance is just a bee
and its sting. Like a bee—
you should see my brothers' bullet
make a comb, by chewing holes
in what is sweet.

My brothers lose
their bullet all the time—
when their bullet takes off on them,
their bullet leaves a hole.

My brothers search their houses,
their bodies for their bullet,
and a little red ghost moans.

Eventually, my brothers call out,
Here, bullet, here—
their bullet comes running, buzzing.
Their bullet always comes
back to them. When their bullet comes
back to them, their bullet
leaves a hole.

My brothers are too slow
for their bullet
because their bullet is in a hurry
and wants to get the lead out.

My brothers' bullet is dressed
for a red carpet
in a copper jacket.

My brothers tell their bullet,
*Careful you don't hurt somebody
with all that flash.*

My brothers kiss their bullet
in a dark cul-de-sac, in front
of the corner store ice machine,
in the passenger seat of their car,
on a strobe-lighted dance floor.
My brothers' bullet
kisses them back.

My brothers break and dance
for their bullet—the jerk,
the stanky leg. They pop, lock

and drop for their bullet,
a move that has them writhing
on the ground—
the worm, my brothers call it.
Yes, my brothers go all-worm
for their bullet.

My brothers' bullet is registered,
is a bullet of letters—has a PD,
a CIB, a GSW, if they are lucky
an EMT, if not, a Triple 9, a DNR,
a DOA.

My brothers never call the cops
on their bullet and instead pledge
allegiance to their bullet
with hands over their hearts
and stomachs and throats.

My brothers say they would die
for their bullet. If my brothers die,
their bullet would be lost.
If my brothers die,
there's no bullet to begin with—
the bullet is for living brothers.

My brothers' feed their bullet
the way the bulls fed Zeus—
burning, on a pyre, their own
thigh bones wrapped in fat.
My brothers take a knee, bow
against the asphalt, prostrate
on the concrete for their bullet

We wouldn't go so far
as to call our bullet
a prophet, my brothers say.
But my brothers' bullet
is always lit like a night-church.
It makes my brothers holy.
You could say my brothers' bullet
cleans them—the way red ants
wash the empty white bowl
of a dead coyote's eye socket.
Yes, my brothers' bullet
cleans them, makes them
ready for god.

Ha ha ha niggers are the worst

you know like how she would lie down in
her dark cornered room with an old movie
and remember again just how normal just
everyday just cold just buck wild casual just
sidewalk crack each smack in the face was
just every day buried in every part of speech
just life and she was just all in it you too
you'd just go ha ha ha niggers are the worst
remember and not even stop to think about
why her stomach hurt how come she had all
that pain in her side or the side of her head
why she needs new glasses just ha ha ha
niggers are the worst and sometimes she
stood big as a house and sometimes she was
a house and the neighbors wished she'd keep
her blinds closed please wished she'd pick
up and move please but there's so much to
lift so much to move   what she's not
allowed to say   i'm lonely   what she's
not allowed to say   this is hard   what
she's not allowed to say   i wish someone
would hold me would let me hold them for
just one full minute   what she's not
allowed to do   cry where we can see her
and laugh   ha ha ha   ha ha ha   ha ha ha
niggers are the worst   remember?   ha ha
ha   ha ha ha   ha ha ha   ha ha ha nig-

DAWN LUNDY MARTIN

EXCERPT FROM Discipline

People are fond of saying, "Everything happens for a reason," which is complete bullshit. Required reading dots the bookshelf. There's Fanon breathing holes into us. And my brother reading in the halty sidesteps of a grade schooler. I know what my brother smells like when he's sick, angling for air, his body deep in the sweat of acquiescence. I want him to be someone else. My father liked to blame any crime in our neighborhood on "American blacks." When he mumbled under his breath, I think he was saying "Goddamned niggers," but I can't be sure.

tatiana de la tierra

Ode to Unsavory Lesbians

i love an ugly lesbian
one who walks with a limp
talks with a lisp
leaves her dentures out overnight by the bathroom sink
wears polyester pants and men's cologne, the cheap kind
has a beard so long she steps on it
sprouts warts on her toes, all twelve of them
carries a spittoon in her breast pocket
chortles at church people

i dream of a lesbian who's always broke
she doesn't own a car, walks
streets barefoot, near and far
washes all her clothes by hand
steals from wal-mart
scams business-suited man
lights matches on her wooden leg
barbeques freshly plucked birds on her shopping cart
seasons them with salt, that's all
licks her fingers in the moonlight

i crave a lesbian who's fat and fleshy
so big she can't fit through the door at starbucks
and they set up an outdoor café just for her
so fat she wears bangles on her fingers
her belly is a boom box
her stretch marks are hieroglyphic etchings

she's so heavy, tectonic plates shift beneath her feet
so huge, lake erie is her bathtub

i lust after an unsavory lesbian
she blows away my lackluster day
leads me in a lambada, lights
lantern between my legs
lays my head down on lace pillows
humps me like a lamppost
lacerates me with leather lust
lacquers my body with blue latex paint
logs the forest for prime wood
builds me lakeside throne

sets me there and worships me
—goddess in blue—
lines my path with ladyslippers
ravishes me with sex words
pets me like little lamb

wins me by landslide

JOSHUA JENNIFER ESPINOZA

I Dream of Horses Eating Cops

i dream of horses eating cops
i have so much hope for the future

or no i don't

who knows the sound a head makes when it is asleep
my dad was a demon but so was the white man in uniform
who harassed him for the crime of being brown

there are demons everywhere
dad said
and he was right but not in the way he meant it

the sky over san bernardino was a brilliant blue when the
winds kicked in
all the fences and trash cans and smog scattered themselves
and the mountains were on fire every day

i couldn't wait to die or be killed
my woman body trapped in a dream

i couldn't wait to wake up
and ride off into the sunset
but there isn't much that's new anywhere

the same violence swallows itself and produces bodies
and names for bodies

i name my body girl of my dreams
i name my body proximity
i name my body full of hope despite everything
i name my body dead girl who hasn't died yet

i hope i come back as an elephant
i hope we all come back as animals
and eat our fill

i hope everyone gets everything they deserve

thirst

but i can't stand not to be swallowed whole,
to be sunken into, wrapped in wet walls

& then broken down, & then dissolved
into someone else's cells. to be craved so hard

i become marrow. stomach lining & tooth.
to be devoured—though not

by a man who expects a meal of me. not by a man
who plucks thighs from street corners, hungers for poultry

to cure his own smallness. those men
i want keeled over & panting on the back steps,

clawing at the screen. those men i wish desert. saltwater.
flat tire in the canyon. wandering the empty shelves

after we fruit have escaped to feast
on each other's pulp, mouths wild & dripping,

hands sticky til we're slick pits, stripped
& sated & ready to return to the soil, ready

to grow our new bodies.

The Clouds Can't Hold Shit

I understand forgiveness, but I have no current desire. When I'm at home, I sleep in the same bed since I was 8. Same fibers in the mattress. I can't smell her, she came before my parents bought the bed, princess beds, as they were advertised.

If you lift the body or liberate the body, it don't matter if you think about their product, the product of them, if you think about them in terms of multiplication & residual, what's left over from their last time touched, by whom.

The grass on our front lawn is brown as I but we still get it cut. I heard there's a drought, but I haven't seen any dead, so we won't do anything in the remembrance of anything.

Dream the worst ends in that bed. A white guy in a wool coat in the summer shoots me in the kidneys, that kind of thing,

where everyone in my dream is actually me. On occasion, I text older men that wanting me isn't embarrassing, it's a choice & we all choose even

what she did to me back in the day, & we choose & we are cruel & stupid but when I wake up in the morning, there's a sun & a ritual I didn't lose anything. Everyone was alive.

Self Portrait

In the white cream
of my lie,

I swallow warm pennies,

listen to the church bells
in the distance—

So much depends
upon insertion.

Just look at all this
face hunger!

Even my peaches
are obscene.

Don't you hear my name
dissolve like the body

of Christ?

*Siempre salgo
con el Jesús en la boca.*

Always tearing
at the hollyhocks,

always so slick
with summer.

Under the corpulent
clouds,

I feed the birds
of my failures,

so tenderly!

My tongue grows plump
as a greedy slug.

Again and again,

an umbrella
opens inside me.

Orifice of heaven—
the twilight comes

like a soiled miracle,

bright as my own
awful pinkness,

and how like a fever
it dazzles.

Constellated

My friend bought
A star and named that
Star after her boyfriend.
I gaze at the summer sky,
Wondering, "Is that you,
Chuy Gómez?"

Lick My Butt

Lick the dry shit out of my sweaty buttcheeks

I've had my hepatitis shots so it's okay

Lick my butt
cos I'm an angry ethnic fag
& I'm in so much pain
so lick my butt

& the next time
when there's a multicultural extravaganza
& I'm asked for referrals
I can say
        "I know this guy,
        he's really cool,
        he licked my butt."

Lick my butt & tell me about
Michel Foucault's theories of deconstruction
& how it applies to popular culture,
a depressed economy & this overwhelming
tide of alienation.

Lick my butt from the center to the margins
& all the way back again.

Read Noam Chomsky in bed to me & lick my butt.

Lick my butt & give me my Prozac.
Lick my butt & call your mother, she misses you.
Flea-dip the cat & lick my butt.
Recycle & lick my butt.

Lick my butt like you really mean it.
Don't just put your tongue there
because you think it's something you should do
Do it cos you really really want to lick my butt.

My butt didn't always liked to be licked;
on the contrary, it hated anything wet
and sloppy, poking blindly
at its puckered dour grimace.
All it wanted was a nice pat,
an occasional squeeze,
a good warm seat and snug underwear.

It was happy with those,
but then all those other butts started
crashing in on its turf,
on the sidewalks and under my bed,
there were all these butts that said,
      no, demanded,
LICK ME.
My butt got tired of all that shit
& it just had to see what the fuss was all about.

At first it approached
the licking with extreme caution,
making sure all the checks
& balances were clearly present.

Hey — my butt had ever reason to be careful
it knows where it's been;
it's had enough of this bigotry
& poverty & violence
it's been on the wrong end of muggings & bashings
it's been working like a damn dog for years to make ends meet
it's been on the lam, on the block, on the contrary
& on sale for far too long

         so when that first slobber, smack,
slurp found its way into that
crack & up that uptight little asshole
it was like the Gay Pride Parade,
the Ice Capades, the Macy's Thanksgiving Day Parade
and Christmas happening all at once.

Now when I walk down the street
and you see me smiling
it's because I'm imagining
your tongue nestled in my buttcheeks
flicking away like a lizard
in a mad tweak.

Lick my butt & I'll lick yours;
we'll deal with shit of the world later.

Boy with Thorn

(1ST CENTURY BC, BRONZE)

1.
Entered, those shadows spoke his loneliness
like a god.

2.
This was new knowledge. The kind he had little
business knowing. The mere
   risk of it making it
all the more delicious.

3.
A forced-out confession. A forcing-it-in.

4.
Each push, where the blood yawned like an opiate.
Each inch, a hermeneutics of the self.

5.
Would you feed on such hurting, would you drink so much?

6.
Was he so terrible a thing to look at?
But was looked at.

7.

His face chiseled deliberate.
His face, a question gone unanswered—

8.

There could have been a thorn already inside? His tongue.
Scratching its wrongs, speaking its six troubles.

9.

How?

10.

There could have been a thorn already inside? The point in his eye.
What makes the shadows their acutest when they lift and sprawl.

11.

I keep thinking of the thorn as
a marker, scrawler, what shapes the places both excused
    and forbidden
in his body's swamp.

12.

*Violence thou shalt want. Violence thou shalt steal
and store inside.*

13.

This Spinario, Fedele, boy with
a message, a mission; Pickaninny—
    Who would not stop for
damage, the old story goes . . .

14.

Shame, guilt, spleen, woe, shock, and want.

15.

He wanted them gone, I know: all his deeper hurts,
poorer gods, that lush resentment.

16.

But failed. They were greater dark, vials
of mystery, done things.

17.

Take it. Don't you have to learn
to take it, eventually?

18.

I told him the thorn was as a key,
his body a lock.

19.

I made him meet the key up with the lock. Turn.

20.

I told him, *Rickey, turn—*

21.

He did: an anti-chrysalis, a lyric,
which is the piece of a prayer visible.

22.

Until he rewound: a new republic, a kingdom where not savagely
he was king.

23.

Who could bare the wind?

24.

Who could feel the self demanding the self ?

25.

Who could see his honesty? His face more handsome
once the pain combed
   through, combed like a river
too clean for love.

26.

*Violence thou shalt want. Violence thou shalt steal
and store inside.*

27.

He would devour it.

28.

This was his body, his body
finally his.

29.

He shut the thorn up in his foot, and told his foot
Walk.

Killing Mark

His plane went down over Los Angeles
last week (again), or was it Long Island?
Boxer shorts, hair gel, his toothbrush
washed up on the shore at New Haven,
but his body never recovered, I feared.

Monday, he cut off his leg chain sawing—
bled to death slowly while I was shopping
for a new lamp, never heard my messages
on his cell phone: *Where are you? Call me!*
I told him to be careful. He never listens.

Tonight, fifteen minutes late, I'm sure
he's hit a moose on Route 26, but maybe
he survived, someone from the hospital
will call me, give me his room number.
I'll bring his pajamas, some magazines.

5:25: still no phone call, voice mail full.
I turn on the news, wait for the report:
flashes of moose blood, his car mangled,
as I buzz around the bedroom dusting
the furniture, sorting the sock drawer.

Did someone knock? I'm expecting
the sheriff by six o'clock. *Mr. Blanco,
I'm afraid* . . . he'll say, hand me a Ziploc

with his wallet, sunglasses, wristwatch.
I'll invite him in, make some coffee.

6:25: I'll have to call his mom, explain,
arrange to fly the body back. Do I have
enough garbage bags for his clothes?
I *should* keep his ties—but his shoes?
Order flowers—roses—white or red?

By seven-thirty I'm taking mental notes
for his eulogy, suddenly adorning all
I've hated, ten years worth of nose hairs
in the sink, of lost car keys, of chewing
too loud and hogging the bedsheets,

when Joey yowls, ears to the sound
of footsteps up the drive, and darts
to the doorway. I follow with a scowl:
Where the hell were you? Couldn't call?
Translation: *I die each time I kill you.*

JULIAN TALAMANTEZ BROLASKI

in the cut

his being punished / for talking Indian.
> —Cedar Sigo, 'Prince Valiant'

person of clear salt water
warm clear deer

the mosquitoes I am
delicious to them
because of my fairy
or my indian blood

he is immune
to poison ivy
because indians dont
call it poison

utter unfaith in humanity
the leaves don't turn right
the leaves so that
they don't know how to turn right

when the guy at the bodega
complained about white ppl & gentrifications
you said me and my friend are native

I'm Suquamish, look it up

I vaporize the weed
we had for breakfast when
I come home from the poetry reading
thinking how low & how lively
we know of the cut

droppd my parasol in a ditch
pretend it didn't happen

Tyler, Texas

      2 out of towners
                in the sharp grasses
         white churches
not a hair feels out of place
         They say the next county over
                from Smith is wet
You go around Ben Wheeler
Through dumb-fuck White House
Back over Black Beauty Ravine
           Drink till mothers due
         back at the home (for memory care)
for a random viewing of Eastside-Westside, 1949
       (Where Stanwyck and Ava Gardner step into the
       same picture)
Finally alone together
       more arrowhead hunting
         We are fuses left scorched under lavender skies
              where Karen Carpenter's longest note
        is broken in half. Near dark I shot what I thought
     was a long stick
and didn't check back for two days
         It was a water moccasin
        head all blown off
      and caved in
         slick as snot

ALICE MOORE DUNBAR-NELSON

You! Inez!

Orange gleams athwart a crimson soul
Lambent flames; purple passion lurks
In your dusk eyes.
Red mouth; flower soft,
Your soul leaps up—and flashes
Star-like, white, flame-hot.
Curving arms, encircling a world of love,
You! Stirring the depths of passionate desire!

EDUARDO C. CORRAL

To a Straight Man

All zodiac all
      radar your voice
           I carried it
across the Atlantic
      to Barcelona
           I photographed
cathedrals
      cacti mosaic
           salamanders
I even photo-
      graphed my lust
           always
your voice skimming
      a woman's skin
           mattress springs
so noisy so birdlike
      you filled her room
           with cages
camera bright
      in my pocket map
           unfolding
in my mind
      I explored a park
           leaves notched
& enormous
      graffitied boulders
           then
three men

                    tall & clean
closed in
            they broke open
                    my body
with their fists
            insufferable
                    your red wool cap
insufferable the way
            you walked
                    away from me
come back please
            the buttons
                    on your jacket
are finches
            I wanted to yell
                    as you vanished
into a hotel
            to drink with
                    your friends
there was nothing
            more
                    you could do
after my attackers left
            before I got up
                    I touched my face
almost tenderly

Diva Doll

Baby doll. Barbie doll. Mama was a Diva. Mama's baby was a doll. Mama collected dolls. Pretty pink, fluffy glamorous porcelain dolls. Mama dressed dolls, dressed me like I was her doll. Fluffy, pretty powder pink show and tell baby doll/ baby girl/mama's baby's girl. Mama loved how dolls looked. Pretty porcelain faces. Ruby lips/ Ebony eyeliner/cinnamon blush. Perfect. Exteriors look pretty/ pink/ shiny/ glossy. Cameras loved mama as much as she loved cameras. Mama shared legacy. Diva doll. Baby doll. Mama's living doll. "Smile real pretty for the camera baby," "Walk down the runway baby girl." Follow mama, follow footsteps, follow Diva. Mama didn't see her baby. Mama saw pink ruffled ponytails. Mama dressed me pretty like her dolls. Everything plastic / coated / covered / perfect show and tell. Mama loved things she could show and tell. Shiny surfaces. Exteriors. Kept dolls wrapped in plastic boxes. Trophies. Show and tell. Mama took pictures/ mama loved studio shots/mama's baby had to sit for studio shots. "Smile pretty baby. Smile like mama. You look like a living doll." Pictures don't lie. Mama didn't see eyes. Peering out. Sad. Empty eyes peering out behind porcelain. Mama hung pictures of baby girl/baby doll/Diva doll all around the house. Mama hung pictures of herself around the house. Living dolls. Pretty pictures filled shelves/walls/empty spaces. Mama's baby doll. Mama's mirror. Mama didn't touch. Taffeta ruffles, bubble gum pink clothes filled closets. Mama covered her baby girl with layers of ruffles, bows, powder pink fluff. Mama didn't touch. Kept
    her in the plastic box.

suicide note #1

in this dream, my father is dead.
i pour alcohol down your spine—
slender canal—and your house flowers
with music. this is some kind of funeral.
you swat your eyelashes
when you want a kiss. my lips are fake.
i take them off, garnish the edge
of my wine glass. the bartender's tattoo
is my home address. i visit his mouth
at the end of the dream. he asks
about sadness. i don't move.
i don't want to move. my father watches
me through the bartender's
muted eyes, says *stay safe*. i can't. i'm black.
i stammer outside, lipless, a siren
searching for destruction.
this is some disease, you say,
enter me slowly. everybody
is watching, raises their wine
to my father's death. that gets you off.
the disease, i whisper in your ear,
is osteoarthritis. it takes you from the inside.
you feel its tail roping my dna, crossing out
cartilage. a need for home. that keeps you
afloat. i lean back into you the way
the city storms. i'm from here.
this is where i was born,

point to your pelvis. you rise.
my father stays put when the water
beads down his new home. lovely coffin.
when my tongue confesses
to the slaughter of black boys,
you speak your condolences.
my father's grave is damp from the rain
and this city ain't worth the gray sky
it paints. i blame my gay, its hunger for men.
the body's dagger. my first mind says
jump. drown. give your bone
before it steals away inside
the tyrant's belly. you push me in.
i thank you.

Survivor 2014

Contrary to what's popular I never liked Diana Nyad
in my mind overrated white woman
ex-olympic swimmer most recently swam from Cuba to Florida
privileged
thrill seeker
daredevil
doing voluntarily what so many people of color
are forced to do while attempting to gain freedom
drowning in boats, falling overboard, terrible accidents,
falling into the jaws of sharks, those waters a meat fest
for predators, slavers
Sometimes I think about slavery and think if only those waters
could tell the tale
I've always wanted to say to those people who go on the
        reality-show Survivor for kicks
try being an artist and make it your career choice
or how about a single mother or father trying to raise a family
on minimum wage living in an impoverished area
try being someone who comes to America and
doesn't speak the language whose entire survival rests upon
learning english
arriving in a strange land, on strange soil, estranged from
        everything
you have ever known
like hitting your head against a glass door, or mirrors
like optical illusions that used to be in the old fun houses
or how about being uninsured and being sick for a number

of years
weathering that storm
or insured but burdened with a costly illness
health plans don't cover
or like so many of my students who are bullied to the point
they have nowhere to turn and no longer have knowledge
of their own name
No I never liked Diana Nyad
until one day I caught a clip of her on Ellen
I caught the part where she talked about her friendship
with Superman Christopher Reeve who in real life suffered
paralysis from the neck down.
He looked at her in later years after she'd retired from swimming
said he feared she wasn't living her own dreams, that
she was an Olympian
And something about her conversations with him motivated her
to try again, to listen.
Maybe through her I saw the frayed ends of my own un-lived dreams,
my own fear that caused paralysis
And so by the end of that conversation with Ellen
where Diana talked about returning to her Olympic Self
by swimming from Cuba to Florida at age 60 challenging
every notion of what it means to be an athlete, a woman,
and the stereotypes of aging I was crying
by the time she looked into the camera and said
Never give up
Don't ever give up on your dreams

RICK BAROT

Wright Park

There must be drugs in the backpack
lying on the grass. One cop is leading away

the bicycle, while the other cops stand around
the man handcuffed on the ground,

not moving but clearly not hurt, waiting
like everyone else for what will happen next.

It's just one faggot on a bicycle,
says the old man holding a cane, standing near,

why so many cops? The park is beautiful
at dusk. The sky a blue-gray dome,

the lawns like billiard tables. The hundred
trees exhale a good, cool air.

The statue of Henrik Ibsen looks out over
the pond's mallards, the dog-walkers,

the teenagers smoking on the benches.
I know the mind's violence, and what I see

is an old man in a blue ski jacket
on a summer evening, his cane thin and white

as a toothpick, not stick enough
to beat back the faggots riding into the park

on their bicycles, the faggots in the flower beds,
the faggots in the trees and bushes,

the blue cops who are also faggots,
the faggots splashing into the pond of ducks

and carp, the faggots on the swings,
the faggots, the faggots everywhere, the faggots.

Consulting the Bones

Surveyor, take note of this happy reunion: pelvis
finds biological torso. Absent years and then this peculiar find.
The return after continental slips. Thin lives punctuated in transit.
One grew a second tongue. Flesh lost to labor, the other.
They have known cold machines. Promises of gold, anchorage,
sweet morsels of God. Their parts unwilling
to fit, will not lock in gaps and jutted wings. Wholeness
was never made for enduring bodies. We have buried
too many of them. Rickety homes, newborn
mouth wide as entrance. Beyond one terminal is another.
Soon, one forgets the taste of sky. There are only small
pleasures now: floor to kneel, one anthem, engorged tit.
Reason to want. There is fatigue in this history,
and passing. There is repetition and passing.

Heavy

The narrow clearing down to the river
I walk alone, out of breath

my body catching on each branch.
Small children maneuver around me.

Often, I want to return to my old body
a body I also hated, but hate less

given knowledge.
Sometimes my friends—my friends

who are always beautiful & heartbroken
look at me like they know

I will die before them.
I think the life I want

is the life I have, but how can I be sure?
There are days when I give up on my body

but not the world. I am alive.
I know this. Alive now

to see the world, to see the river
rupture everything with its light.

DERRICK AUSTIN

The Lost Woods as Elegy for Black Childhood

There used to be no one here,
where cypresses and oaks play
shadow puppets on sawgrass.

You heard the music before
I did: tambourines, pan pipes.
Remember how I woke clean

to meet you each morning?
The dew and the dust?
Remember how you'd catch me

as I fell from trees? Someone
heard and hurt us. I'm Black-Eyed
Pea. You're just Skull Kid.

We wanted our genius to last.
We never wanted chalkboards
or snow. We never came home

before the streetlights buzzed.
All we do is dance in leaves.
Cackle and Dreaming, we call it.

Our mothers call it grief.

Self-Portrait as a Door

All the birds die of blunt force trauma—
of barn of wire of *YIELD* or *SLOW*
CHILDREN AT PLAY. You are a sign
are a plank are a raft are a felled oak.
You are a handle are a turn are a bit
of brass lovingly polished.
What birds what bugs what soft
hand come knocking. What echo
what empty what room in need
of a picture a mirror a bit of paint
on the wall. There is a hooked rug
There is a hand hard as you are hard
pounding the door. There is the doormat
owl eye patched by a boot by a body
with a tree for a hand. What roosts
what burrows what scrambles
at the pound. There is a you
on the other side, cold and white
as the room, in need of a window
or an eye. There is your hand
on the door which is now the door
pretending to be a thing that opens.

Last Words of the Honey Bees

Honey, our hive is built and ruled
by women. Honey, we were once *wild*.
Honey, look at the flowers. We raised
them into artichoke, pepper, squash,
and apple for you, Honey. You found
our hive and renamed it *colony*—or
a factory of Yellow, Black, and Brown
honey—we are the silent workers
who bring home your dinner,
whether or not our Honey comes home.
Home was the wild flower you pulled
out to plant your White monoculture.
Honey, we pollinate thirty acres of White
apple trees to bring home one pound
of honey, to bring home one pound
of bodies. The poison in the pollen
is poison in our colony is poison
in your children. Honey, tell me:
was your breakfast sweet? Honey,
when this colony collapses into a pool
of Yellow Black and Brown honey,
the women are always the first to go.
I close my wings and hit the ground.
I open my wings and my colony
drops dead. I close my wings
and every flower at my funeral
begins to grieve. Honey?

Who will raise the flowers
when we are gone? Honey,
do you see our queen?
She is next. And then
the Earth, and you,
Honey. Every drop
of my Yellow
Black & Brown
is falling into
a feld of
White.

Honey,
I'm home.

hyena (an absolution chant for the beloved community)

ashe ashe ashe
ashe how you say
ashe ashe ashe
ashe why you say
ashe ashe ashe
ashe which you
say ashe ashe ashe
ashe what you say
who you say

ohkay ohkay ohkay
ohkay how you do
ohkay ohkay ohkay
ohkay why you do
ohkay ohkay ohkay
ohkay which you do
ohkay ohkay ohkay
ohkay what you do
who you do

ayo ayo ayo
ayo why you want
ayo ayo ayo ayo
how you want
ayo ayo ayo ayo
which you want

ayo ayo ayo ayo
what you want
who you want

kikikiki kikikiki
kikikiki how you lie
kikikiki kikikiki
kikikiki which you lie
kikikiki kikikiki
kikikiki what you lie
kikikiki kikikiki
kikikiki why you lie
who you lie

olu olu olu olu
what you kill
olu olu olu olu
why you kill
olu olu olu olu
which you kill
olu olu olu olu
how you kill
who you kill

shalom shalom shalom
shalom why you hide
shalom shalom shalom
shalom how you hide
shalom shalom shalom
shalom which you hide
shalom shalom shalom
shalom what you hide
who you hide

selah selah selah selah
what you let down
selah selah selah selah
which you let down
selah selah selah selah
why you let down
selah selah selah selah
how you let down who
you let down

ye ye ye yemanya
why you trouble
ye ye ye yemanya
how you trouble
ye ye ye yemanya
what you trouble
ye ye ye yemanya
which you trouble
who you trouble

wadi wadi wadi
wadi which you love
wadi wadi wadi
wadi how you love
wadi wadi wadi
wadi why you love
wadi wadi wadi
wadi what you love
who you love

To the American Psychiatric Association – 1973

I woke this morning
no longer crazy.
No difference in the mirror just
a breath slipping from me
soft as a bird in flight

I'd gone to bed uneasy in my madness,
the burden of perversity an unstable pillow.
The lover at my side lies
restless with her diagnosis too.

The symptoms thrust like shadows
across the wall of a top floor room,
concealing themselves in the
density of light.

I heard voices, disembodied
rising like smoke from the wood
stacked tight at the bottom of a stake.

Visions, seditious things
that were not there: a woman
with her hand in another's,
gripping firmly, holding on for life;
me inside a golden window light
with others. Always others.

Clad only in diaphanous silks
Or thick binding layers
we screamed obscenities at passersby
cataloguing imagined inequities:

Anti-social, anti-colonial, anti-patriarchy,
Anti-racist, anti-sexist, anti-capitalist,
Anti-establishment
even when they strapped
my arms to my sides
and claimed I was incurable.

Then I woke this morning,
no longer just that crazy lesbian
footnoted in the texts.
But a feminist who's still quite angry.

VII

I like to walk beside you, treading
your shadow along the way,
letting your steps mark my steps,
follow you like a boat being towed—

fitting my feet in the footprints
you leave like a puma on the sand,
I want to be the towel that dries you,
the one you spread to sunbathe

how lucky: the belt that gets to hug
your waist, the crucifix that hangs
from a chain on your chest!

what joy: to arrive every day as a comb
and smell the morning in your hair
but rather than comb, uncomb you!

The Language of Dust

"From grave to grave
I carry my loyalty to you."
                    —*Essex Hemphill*

where
do you find
strength
to climb
down the hill
to your lover's
grave

what
do you bring
but thirteen years
of memories/

how do you deal
with his death
when your gasps
loom
in the autumn air
like circling crows
spasms rock
your body
like squirrels
shake the scarlet oak

& purple dogwood
branches
while through the buzz
of a helicopter
the roar
of an elevated train
the firecracker thunder
of a buddhist service
one can still hear
your sobs
over & over
utter his name/

jan
my jan
even blindfolded
i would find my way
to you
around this
evergreen cemetery

i gaze at
the engraved picture/
I outline
the entwined hearts/
i smooth out
the act-up triangle/

the musical notes
float high
on each side
of your Viking name

along with dates of birth
& recent death/
poetry books

flap bold
on each side
of my voodoo pseudonym
birth name & date
open-ended/

i smile at
the "nuclear lover" epitaph/
i sit on
the grass grateful
i will rest
not soon enough
right here
above you
in the shadow
of the trade center
towering
in the distance/

years ago
after we found out
our status
i begged you
to be buried
with me
because i don't believe
in the foolishness
of spiritual
afterlife

"the soul survives"
you insisted/

"prove it"
i demanded/

"man is the only creature
known to bury its dead"
you persisted/

"should we act
like dogs & swine"
i contended/

"manhattan queens
why should we be buried
of all places in Brooklyn"
you retorted/

as usual
my patience thinned fast/
hysterical i screamed
if you died before me
i could not carry out
your wish to be
cremated/

at first
you laughed
that you would
outlast me
then guessing

the improbability
you lashed back
that i always need
to have things my way

threatening
to replace me
as your executioner/

hurt
i held you hard
as you tried
to break away
from my embrace
while cross my heart
i swore
to do right by you/
there was this masochist
ex-priest
who after his love's
cremation
adding a dash of ash
to the dough
every sunday baked a batch
of peanut butter cookies
as he listened to mass
on the road/

with no more communion
to down as morning pick-me-up
to sweeten afternoon naps
to soothe nightmares

he dressed in a harness
knelt in the bathtub
slashed his wrists letting
his blood drop
in the urn
while on the cd
callas repeatedly sobbed
"vissi d'arte vissi d'amore"/

drama queen
he reminded me
of something
i would do
like that midday
in summer
i freaked
pulled out my dick
jerked off quick
on the geraniums
over the grave/

i also remember
during my second hospitalization
we watched
this television report
on greedy companies
that cremate corpses
together
& handed families
the wrong remains/

open-mouth shaken
you paced the room
we shared in co-op care/
laid down with p.c.p.
my throat got tight/

then last year
in the candlelight glow
of a swedish meatballs
haitian rice & beans
anniversary dinner
capped with entenmann's eclairs
you affirmed to be buried with me
would honor our relationship/

that night
we curled
into each other
aware
one of us
would leave roses
tears & kisses
on our tombstone
the next november 9th/

Kindertotenlieder

After midnight everything becomes musical
like the names of flowers: names of diseases, for
example, like pneumocystis

carinii pneumonia blossoming in your lungs,
its petals of infection closing the breath. I wouldn't want
to make that beautiful, a self-congratulating sadness

in my blood. There are numbers of flowers
suitable for funerals whose names I don't know, many
of them toxic if ingested. Rinse the affected area

thoroughly with cold water, irrigate
the blood: surely something will grow there, something
has to. The body is surely no grave. Like

Kaposi's sarcoma, harsh syllables pronounced
across the skin, the purple lesions almost
hyacinth. No death is quite so flower-like, the god
           (who was

in love, remember) turning away so not to spoil the
           composition.
From that boy's blood a single flower sprang, the gardens
of Adonis which wither within a week. I hate

the stupid flowers stealing youth. Beauty

is not an infection, contagion is no bloom upon the
        cheek, the thorn
that takes the rose into the true. The death

of beauty is diagnosed by no flower. How afraid I am
of your outstretched hand, its petals
white and black and falling fingers.

Heartbeats

Work out. Ten laps.
Chin ups. Look good.

Steam room. Dress warm.
Call home. Fresh air.

Eat right. Rest well.
Sweetheart. Safe sex.

Sore throat. Long flu.
Hard nodes. Beware.

Test blood. Count cells.
Reds thin. Whites low.

Dress warm. Eat well.
Short breath. Fatigue.

Night sweats. Dry cough.
Loose stools. Weight loss.

Get mad. Fight back.
Call home. Rest well.

Don't cry. Take charge.
No sex. Eat right.

Call home. Talk slow.
Chin up. No air.

Arms wide. Nodes hard.
Cough dry. Hold on.

Mouth wide. Drink this.
Breathe in. Breathe out.

No air. Breathe in.
Breathe in. No air.

Black out. White rooms.
Head hot. Feet cold.

No work. Eat right.
CAT scan. Chin up.

Breathe in. Breathe out.
No air. No air.

Thin blood. Sore lungs.
Mouth dry. Mind gone.

Six months? Three weeks?
Can't eat. No air.

Today? Tonight?
It waits. For me.

Sweet heart. Don't stop.
Breathe in. Breathe out.

EXCERPT FROM **A Song of Someplace Yet to Fall**

4.

But I am not cruelty-free. I do not offer a gluten-free option.

I won't talk like a pirate. I won't pump up the volume, get wasted, have sex with you at Burning Man. I won't dig your hip-hop, save the planet at this badass rally, talk Chinese, support your Greenpeace, stop eating sushi forsake animal proteins watch Glee ride a fixiedonatetoIndiegogoleggoyourEggo.

I start my Honda, drive
to my favorite freezer section
soft-shoe past the okra and peas,
waltz by the Breyers
Caramel Praline Crunch.

You miss Chik-Fil-A?
I am my own guilty pleasure.

The security guard, the cashier,
even the cart with one stuck wheel
cannot stop the revel
of this nighttime promenade.

Twenty years ago, the astrologer
would not suspend his disbelief.
Ten years ago, the composer
could not harmonize
transgender with friend.
Five years ago the weaver
unraveled a rainbow at my name.

Someday my car
won't pass the smog test.
Just found out I may go blind.
Each day I take five pills
to make me be a little more
like something I can never be.

Someone may mark me
with bad weather and omens.
Judgment might thread through
the foot-treadle stars.

Yet I will hear hummingbirds,
sip my coffee, maybe sit on an ice chest.

Until her saviors go away.
Until her spirit guide stops
reciting every reason to kneel

before the next muscle
car blowing down her street,

who can ponder which witch
she has become,
yet how completely she still
would give her dance to love?

KAZIM ALI

His Last Stand

Mouth filling with rain
Creature of fire on the roof before the storm
The window in the ceiling opens to light I thrum
Last chapter I ever learned by heart
Lonely in the house below
I still believe
But have no reason at all to speak
With no more riches than a couple of stones
Cast out or cast down
What do I know about sacred books or men
Nothing

Boy in a Stolen Evening Gown

In this field of thistle, I am the improbable
lady. How I wear the word: sequined weight
snagging my saunter into overgrown grass, blonde
split-end blades. I waltz in an acre of bad wigs.

Sir who is no one, sir who is yet to come, I need you
to undo this zipped back, trace the chiffon
body I've borrowed. See how I switch my hips

for you, dry grass cracking under my pretend
high heels? Call me and I'm at your side,
one wildflower behind my ear. Ask me
and I'll slip out of this softness, the dress

a black cloud at my feet. I could be the boy
wearing nothing, a negligee of gnats.

REN HANG
TRANSLATED BY **HO KING MAN** *AND* **CASEY ROBBINS**

Each time I did something bad

yesterday I being in the supermarket
stole a tube of toothpaste
day before yesterday with gum
plugged up the neighbor's keyhole
last week flipped over
the full row of trash cans
from the building entrance
each time I did something bad
already it felt like life
returned to better some

RACHEL ELIZA GRIFFITHS

ambition

the birds fell
dead in our front yards
new crosses of agnostics
our father who art plagued
we chewed the barred
owl's wings
they fell into our pulpits
bald plucked dipped
heathen drunk in oil they fell
eyeless in the sand
they were at whole foods
falling into bags of rice
imported GMO
we can't outgrow
ourselves
whatever the buzzards
leave of claw

the great eagle

KAMILAH AISHA MOON

Watching a Woman on the M101 Express

You sit in a hard blue seat, one
of the ones reserved for the elderly
or infirm, a statue of need. Your mouth

open as if waiting for water or medicine, as if
mugged mid-sentence, or some ice age hit
right after terrible news.

Oblivious to the Metro's bump and buck,
to the toddler begging in Spanish to be freed
from her stroller, to my ogling, you sit

embalmed, raccooned or moosed. You have
the kind of eyes that never quite close,
even in deepest sleep, lids

an undersized t-shirt that leaves belly
exposed. Tears navigate moles, veteran
swimmers of your creek-bed face.

I can't stop looking. You can't get over
whatever has happened, so shell-shocked
that birds could land and roost. I want to ask—

just so you know someone
is paying attention, but not enough
to know what ravages. It's rude

to stare. I'm from the South, a suburb
where Grief pulls the shades first,
stays home if indecent. But

your sorrow struts four rows down
from me, strands you an astronaut
on some distant, undiscovered moon.

Bodies to your left and right read papers,
nap, send text messages. You sit in a hard
blue seat, mouth open. I study the pink

of your jaw, and wonder if you'll come back
before your stop comes.

RIGOBERTO GONZÁLEZ

The Bordercrosser's Pillowbook

things that shine in the night

Fulgencio's silver crown—when he snores
the moon, coin of Judas, glaring
at the smaller metals we call stars
my buckle
the tips of my boots
the stones in my kidneys
an earring
a tear on the cheek
the forked paths of a zipper
the blade of the pocketknife triggering open
the blade of the pocketknife seducing the orange
the blade of the pocketknife salivating
the blade of the pocketknife
the word México
the word migra

things that are afraid to move when they sleep

the owls carved on rock
Fulgencio
me

things that forget their shapes

snakes
our bedding
our clothes
the shadows twitching by the fire
the skin of the rabbit—its flesh
an apple
the orange
the jacaranda behind the house
the roof—the clothsline—the curtains
the door that swells in the heat
the pipes that shrink in the cold
the couch—the table—the lamp
the dominoes
the dishes
the children—the wife—the neighbors
memory

things that make noises at dawn

the sun as it rips away from the horizon
the sun as it pounds against my skin
the sand moaning with my weight
my weight moaning with the sand
the stones in my kidneys
children waking up in the homes we left behind
the footfalls—the footprints—the foot
Fulgencio's prayer without saints—or God

things that open like flowers in daylight

Fulgencio's eyes
Fulgencio's mouth—as he yawns
the buttons on his shirt
the orange peel—the campsite—the desert—the world
the jacaranda behind the house
the roof—the clothesline—the curtains
the door that swells in the heat
the pipes that shrink in the cold
the couch—the table—the lamp
the dominoes
the dishes
the children—the wife—the neighbors
memory
the white sparks in my brain
the red sparks in my heart
the stones in my kidneys

things that travel at the speed of silence

air
sand
heat
light
grief
memory
thought
Fulgencio
me

things I would say to Fulgencio if I could say them

erase our shadows
carve our names in stone
let us watch for comets while we rest
let us not make wishes that will not come true
your shoes abandoned you the way I never will
let me fan the fires on your toes
these are the final drops of my fear—drink them
these are the final drops of my fever—drink them
these are the final drops of my love—drink them
hold me—I have a flame on my tongue
hold me—you are a mouth of water
hold me—we taste of tangerines
hold me

things I want to polish clean

an apple—and another one—and another
my buckle
the tips on my boots
Fulgencio's forehead
our tracks on the sand
the ring on my finger
the horizon—its infestation of green cars
the word wetback
the voice—the bullhorn—the officer
Fulgencio's tears of shame—the sores on his toes
the sound of static—of running motors—of running men
the jacaranda behind the house
the rood—the clotheslines—the curtains
the door that swells in the heat
the pipes that shrink in the cold
the couch—the table—the lamp
the dominoes
the dishes
the children—the wife—the neighbors
memory
the stones in my kidneys
the stones in my kidneys
I'd set them in gold—
I'd set them in gold—try to wear them like teeth

EMANUEL XAVIER

Step Father

He forgets that he used to call me *mariconcito*-
that I harbored years of hatred toward him
while hoping to find my real father. My
childhood memories of him reminding me
I was my mother's son, not his. I tried
to poison him once and scattered sharp nails
inside the shoes in his closet. By the time one
of his sons died of AIDS I was already lost
in contempt for the man I blamed for everything.
There was the time I was in love and he met my
boyfriend. Now he forgets to go to the bathroom

or where he is but he still remembers Michael
and asks about him. I help him walk slowly
outdoors to step outside the prison cell that is
the tiny apartment with no windows in which
I grew up abused by both of them. He barely
understands. His fate has been torture. I know
that I cannot be his savior. I used to pray for
him to die but here he is slowly fading. In his
eyes I see that he learned to love me and wishes
he could take it all back. He is unable to recall
those drunken nights and hateful words. I should

do the same. I left a long time ago but he still
remains haunted by the little boy who wanted
to belong. Like him, I want to forget that we

made mistakes and caused so much pain. I need for both of us to remember how he taught me how to ride a bike and how to swim and told me, better late than never, that he loved me and was proud of all I had done. I have to help him settle into his favorite chair and let him know that I forgive him. There is a place somewhere where he will call me *hijo* and I will know him as my dad.

CHARIF SHANAHAN

At *L'Express* French Bistro My White Father Kisses My Black Mother Then Calls the Waiter a Nigger

I change the subject and ask
How long
He thinks he'll run.
He says, *Son, I am complete*
To the bone. I say, *You're evading my question.*

He says, *How's the job?*
Mom says, *Tell me how you feel.*
These days, I mutter, *black. Quite black. Pass the cream.*
He says, *What do you mean?*

To the waiter Mom says, *Bien cuit*
S'il vous plaît, smiling.
I say, *He doesn't speak French.*
Mom says, *On parle français au Maroc.* I say,
Yes, Mom, in Senegal too.

PAULA GUNN ALLEN

Some Like Indians Endure

dykes remind me of Indians
like Indians dykes
are supposed to die out
or forget
or drink all the time
or shatter
go away
to nowhere
to remember what will happen
if they don't

they don't
anyway
even though it
happens
and they remember
they don't

because the moon remembers
because so does the sun
because so do the stars
remember
and the persistent stubborn
grass
of the earth

Cattails

One woman drives across five states just to see her. The woman being driven to has no idea anyone's headed her way. The driving woman crosses three bridges & seven lakes just to get to her door. She stops along the highway, wades into the soggy ground, cuts down coral-eyed cattails, carries them to her car as if they might be sherbet orange, long-stemmed, Confederate roses, sheared for Sherman himself. For two days she drives toward the woman in Kentucky, sleeping in rest areas with her seat lowered all the way back, doors locked. When she reaches the state line it's misting. The tired pedal-to-the-metal woman finally calls ahead. *I'm here,* she says. *Who's this?* The woman being driven to, who has never checked her oil, asks. The driving woman reminds her of the recent writing workshop where they shared love for all things out-of-doors and lyrical. *Come, have lunch with me,* the driving woman invites. They eat spinach salads with different kinds of dressing. They talk about driving, the third thing they both love and how fast clouds can change from state line to state line. The didn't-know-she-was-coming woman stares at she who has just arrived. She tries to read the mighty spinach leaves in her bowl, privately marveling at the driving woman's muscled spontaneity. She can hardly believe this almost stranger has made it across five states just to have lunch with her. She wonders where this mad driving woman will sleep tonight. She is of two driving minds. One convertible. One hardtop. The driving woman shows her pictures of her children. Beautiful, the other does not say. Before long words run out of petrol. The woman who is home, but without pictures of her own, announces she must go. The driving woman frets &

flames, *May I walk you to your car?* They walk. The driver changes two lanes in third gear, fast. The trunk opens. The Mario Andretti look-alike fills the other woman's arms with sable-sheared cattails. Five feet high & badly in need of sunlight & proudly stolen from across five states. The woman with no children of her own pulls their twenty pounds in close, resting them over her Peter-Panning heart. Her lungs empty out, then fill, then fill again with the surge of birth & surprise. For two years, until their velvet bodies begin (and end) to fall to pieces, every time the driven-to woman passes the bouquet of them, there, in the vase by the front door, she is reminded of what falling in love, without permission, smells like. Each time she reaches for her keys, she recalls what you must be willing to turn into for love: spiny oyster mushroom, damson, salt marsh, cedar, creosote, new bud of pomegranate, Aegean sage blue sea, fig, blueberry, marigold, leaf fall, fogs eye, dusty miller, thief-of-the-night.

COUNTEE CULLEN

I Have a Rendezvous With Life

I have a rendezvous with Life,
In days I hope will come,
Ere youth has sped, and strength of mind,
Ere voices sweet grow dumb.
I have a rendezvous with Life,
When Spring's first heralds hum.
Sure some would cry it's better far
To crown their days with sleep
Than face the road, the wind and rain,
To heed the calling deep.
Though wet nor blow nor space I fear,
Yet fear I deeply, too,
Lest Death should meet and claim me ere
I keep Life's rendezvous.

Fuck U's

(In lieu of thank you's, considerin how they luh callin me such ah
ungrateful bitch n all)

Ta evry light-skinned person who thought I was ova-exaggeratin.
Fuck you bitch!
Ta evry dark-skinned person who thought we'd look odd tagetha.
Fuck you bitch!
Ta evry person who raped me like it was sum typa social service.
Fuck you bitch!
Ta evry white person who tol me ta tell my story, but leave out
that whole racism part.
Fuck you bitch!
Ta evry non-black POC who rides my pain like the lone ranger on
nat cot-damn horse.
Fuck you bitch!
Ta evry advocate who only advocates for those who meet your
criteria, n activist who only acts when it's in their best interest.
Fuck you bitch!
Ta evry feminist n womanist who treats/treated me like the
actual man who raped them, all the while slappin my ass n
gropin my titties cuz dey can't believe it's not butta.
Fuck you bitch!
Ta evry elda who thinks wisdom comes from age and not
experience, but can't explain why there are so many old fools.
Fuck you bitch!
Ta evry person in the Trans Movement who deemed me good
enuf to siphon from, mock, n good ole-fashion mammify, but

not worship, love, and properly compensate.

Fuck you bitch!

Ta evry pseudo-intellectual, quasi-revolutionary, fake-deep ass muhfucka who thank a po', dark-skint intersex, gnc, fat femme sayin bitch, is misogynistic cuz they clearly have no sense ah privilege matriculation, n ney systems analysis might as well came outta crack jack box.

Fuck, you bitch!

N ta anybody, who will eva, even contemplate, attempting to oppress me.

Fuck you? In advance.

Enjoy my book!

The Tattooed Man

I gaze at you,
longing, longing,
as from a gilt
and scarlet cage;
silent, speak
your name, cry—
Love me.
To touch you, once
to hold you close—
My jungle arms,
their prized chimeras,
appall. You fear
the birds-of-paradise
perched on my thighs.

Oh to break through,
to free myself—
lifer in The Hole—
from servitude
I willed. Or was
it evil circumstance
that drove me to seek
in strangeness strange
abiding-place?
Born alien,
homeless everywhere,
did I then choose

bizarrity,
having no other choice?

Hundreds have paid
to gawk at me—
grotesque outsider whose
unnaturalness
assures them they
are natural, they indeed
belong.
But you but you,
for whom I would
endure caustic acids,
keenest knives—
you look at me with pain,
avert your face,
love's own,
ineffable and pure
and not for gargoyle
kisses such as mine.

Da Vinci's Last Supper—
a masterpiece
in jewel colors
on my breast
(I clenched my teeth in pain;
all art is pain
suffered and outlived);
gryphons, naked Adam
embracing naked Eve,
a gaiety of imps
in cinnabar;

the Black Widow
peering from the web
she spun, belly to groin—
These that were my pride
repel the union of
your flesh with mine.

I yearn I yearn.
And if I dared
the agonies
of metamorphosis,
would I not find
you altered then?
I do not want
you other than you are.
And I—I cannot
(will not?) change.
It is too late
for any change
but death.
I am I.

ANGELINA WELD GRIMKÉ

El Beso

Twilight—and you
Quiet—the stars;
Snare of the shine of your teeth,
Your provocative laughter,
The gloom of your hair;
Lure of you, eye and lip;
Yearning, yearning,
Languor, surrender;
Your mouth,
And madness, madness,
Tremulous, breathless, flaming,
The space of a sigh;
Then awakening—remembrance,
Pain, regret—your sobbing;
And again, quiet—the stars,
Twilight—and you.

Summer of 1973

Right after I witnessed a phalanx of black lesbians
give a panel on gay liberation,
I fell in love with a spinsterish butch
of a black woman with a Scandinavian first name.
We chased each other every night
all over the West Village,
cruising every woman that walked or rode.
She knew the Upper West Side like the palms
of her talony hands.

We would sit in a subleased apartment
on Columbus Avenue playing double-deck Pinochle
with two other bulldaggers
for three nights straight.

My whole summer was bulldaggers, spinsters,
generous femmes, dark butches, and loud-talking lesbians.

EXCERPT FROM Last Four Months

yo pienso piense
when i started my instagram
i shared my successes
only
didnt think i could
grab help in kind
the
kind i needed
i still dont
my body only
knows
as much as
its
allergic
to
thats squat

an
apparition
awaits
you

i wish i never made any
white friends so many
have demanded a life story
but i only have those
of the dead

i dont trust
cis folks
people
cars men
traffic gas money
id burn them all too
im not always that angry
or beaten down
god
dear diary
im on the bus
where are you
why are you
so sad

i will murder every
last one of you

tylenol inherent
i intro
spect my life
im gone
im done and gone gone and done

darkness
is construct
melanated
warfare

convincible
of
separate
unequal

deatheat
the hands
of the
unprotected

silence is death
140 characters vs a colonic
she died on that
cross too heavy

touch me touch me
dont be sweet
—lady gaga

my boyfriend
is still on grindr
=
fuck that

back to
i give up
dont touch what you cant accord

hate isnt everything

its currency

JAMES BALDWIN

Untitled

Lord,

    when you send the rain

    think about it, please,

    a little?

  Do

    not get carried away

    by the sound of falling water,

    the marvelous light

    on the falling water.

   I

    am beneath that water.

    It falls with great force

    and the light

Blinds

    me to the light.

ACKNOWLEDGEMENTS

Major creators of the *Nepantla* anthology are all queer people of color. William Johnson and Tony Valenzuela, who are the main contacts at Lambda Literary, are both queer people of color. The founder of Nightboat Books, Kazim Ali, is a queer person of color. Also, Irmand Trujillo, who designed the cover of the anthology and created the photograph used on the cover of the anthology is a queer person of color. *Nepantla* was produced with great thanks to the aforementioned individuals.

Thanks should also be given to Lindsey Boldt, Stephen Motika, Andrea Abi-Karam, and everyone else at Nightboat Books who has supported this project with their finances, time, and dedication. Thanks is given to all of the poets, publishers, estates, and family members of the deceased who have allowed permissions for the poems included in this anthology.

Lastly, special thanks to NYU who allowed queer poets of color to meet and discuss the creation of the first online issue of *Nepantla* at the Writer's House, then hosted a portion of *Nepantla*'s first reading series. With thanks to Columbia University, the Audre Lorde Project, Cave Canem, Kundiman, CantoMundo, VIDA, and all other organizations who have also cohosted events and supported the efforts of *Nepantla*. This anthology was made in the memory of all the queer poets of color who left too soon, especially those who chose to end their lives or who were taken away by the AIDS epidemic.

PUBLICATION CREDITS

All poems included in this anthology have been published with permission from the author, publisher, or estate that holds rights to the work. If a poet featured in this anthology does not have their rights listed below, then it means that permission for reproduction of the work was given directly by the poet to the editor of *Nepantla*. Poems within this anthology should not be duplicated or redistributed without the appropriate permissions.

PAT PARKER (1944-1989)
"[I am a child of America]" © 2016 by Anastasia Dunham-Parker-Brady. All rights reserved. Used by permission of Sinister Wisdom, Inc. This poem was not previously titled by Pat Parker and it was titled "[I am a child of America]" by Sinister Wisdom in *The Complete Works of Pat Parker*. For this anthology, Christopher Soto has published the poem under the title "Don't Let the Fascists Speak" because there is an audio recording of Pat Parker available where she uses that title to introduce the poem.

JUNE JORDAN (1936-2002)
"Poem about Police Violence" © 2005 June Jordan Literary Estate trust; reprinted by permission.

AI (1947-2010)
"Riot Act, April 29, 1992" © 1993 by Ai, from *The Collected Poems of Ai* by Ai. Used by permission of W. W. Norton & Company, Inc.

AUDRE LORDE (1934-1992)
"Power" © 1978 by Audre Lorde, from *The Collected Poems Of Audre Lorde* by Audre Lorde. Used by permission of W. W. Norton & Company, Inc.

ADRIAN STANFORD (1942-1981)
"for stan" published with permission from C. Todd White, chair of The Tangent Group. All rights reserved.

BETH BRANT (1941-2015)
"Ride the Turtle's Back" published with permission from Nathanael German, a family member of Beth Brant. All rights reserved.

ESSEX HEMPHILL (1957-1995)
"American Wedding" © Essex Hemphill, used by permission of The Frances Golden Literary Agency, Inc.

DAWN LUNDY MARTIN
Reprinted with permission of Nightboat Books, publisher of *Discipline* by Dawn Lundy Martin (2011). All rights reserved.

tatiana de la tierra (1961-2012)
"Ode to Unsavory Lesbians" published with permission from Olga Garcia and Maylei Blackwell, who hold rights to the work of tatiana de la tierra. All rights reserved.

JUSTIN CHIN (1969-2015)
"Lick My Butt" from *Bite Hard* © 1997 by Justin Chin. Published by Manic D Press. Reprinted by permission of the publisher.

RICHARD BLANCO
"Killing Mark" from *Looking for the Gulf Motel*, by Richard Blanco, © 2012. Reprinted by permission of the University of Pittsburgh Press.

ALICE MOORE DUNBAR-NELSON (1875-1935)
"You! Inez!" is in the public domain.

AKILAH OLIVER (1961-2011)
"Hyena (An Absolution Chant for the Beloved Community)" from *A Toast in the House of Friends*. © 2009 by Akilah Oliver. Reprinted with the permission of The Permissions Company, Inc. on behalf of Coffee House Press.

FRANCISCO X. ALARCÓN (1954-2016)
"VII" published with permission from Javier Pinzon, who holds rights to the work of Francisco X. Alarcón. All rights reserved.

ASSOTTO SAINT (1957-1994)
"The Language of Dust" first appeared in *Wishing for Wings* (Guliens Press) Reprinted with permission by Michele Karlsberg, executor of Assotto Saint's Literary Estate.

REGINALD SHEPHERD (1963-2008)
"Kindertotenlieder" from *Some Are Drowning* by Reginald Shepherd, © 1995. Reprinted by permission of the University of Pittsburgh Press.

MELVIN DIXON (1950-1992)
"Heartbeats" published in *Love's Instruments* by Melvin Dixon, Tia Chucha Press, Los Angeles. All rights reserved.

CHRISTOPHER SOTO is a poet based in Brooklyn. He is the author of *Sad Girl Poems*, cofounder of the Undocupoets Campaign, and editor of *Nepantla: An Anthology*. He received his MFA in Poetry from New York University.

NIGHTBOAT BOOKS

Nightboat Books, a nonprofit organization, seeks to develop audiences for writers whose work resists convention and transcends boundaries. We publish books rich with poignancy, intelligence, and risk. Please visit our website, www.nightboat.org, to learn about our titles and how you can support our future publications.

The following individuals have supported the publication of this book. We thank them for their generosity and commitment to the mission of Nightboat Books:

    Elizabeth Motika
    Benjamin Taylor

In addition, this book has been made possible, in part, by grants from the National Endowment for the Arts and the New York State Council on the Arts Literature Program.